Praise for
STRATEGY TO ACTION

"*Strategy to Action* is exactly that: a practical methodology that will turn your biggest ideas into real offerings in your business and life."

TENDAYI VIKI, author of *Pirates in the Navy* and associate partner at Strategyzer

"*Strategy to Action* is a must-read for entrepreneurs, CEOs, and team leaders seeking to purposefully shape their plan for growth. Keita Demming's Strategy Quadrant framework helps teams identify the tactics needed to start small and intentionally build to reach the long-term goal. Demming shows that what you do in the short term needs to serve your future, and making changes can take several years. Sometimes, the business must make a short-term sacrifice to achieve a considerably larger long-term result. Taking risks requires careful planning, and how to do it is laid out clearly in this book."

HUGH MASSIE, executive chairman and founder of DNA Behavior International

"Keita Demming has written a wonderfully thoughtful and accessible book for all of us who are trying to make a real difference in the world."

ADAM KAHANE, director of Reos Partners and author of *Facilitating Breakthrough*

"*Strategy to Action* is a concise and compelling manifesto for closing the gap between ideas and business results. This book provides tools and inspiration to help entrepreneurs and professionals clarify their business dreams and bring them to life!"

GENA COX, PhD, award-winning author of *Leading Inclusion*

"Keita Demming integrates personal, strategic, and operational perspectives well. He provides us with thoughtful guidance so we can move beyond ideation to implementation. The book is focused, well-written, and uses examples that are vivid and powerful."

ANN ARMSTRONG, PhD, director of ICUBE, IMI at University of Toronto Mississauga

"Are you ready to bridge the gap between strategy and tactics, shape your future, and make your business dreams a reality? If so, this book is your ultimate guide."

DAVID BURKUS, author of *Best Team Ever*

"*Strategy to Action* describes how to design the business that is right for you so you can leverage systems, processes, and approaches to drive revenue. Keita Demming is passionate about helping entrepreneurs and leaders become better business people and better people in business. Keita provides real-life examples, stories, and analogies to illustrate how you convert ideas into measurable results."

NORM TRAINOR, president and CEO of The Covenant Group

"I *like* executing tactics that have meaningful, measurable results. But I *love* strategy and all it entails. I often questioned if the two aligned—until I was given a copy of *Strategy to Action*. It is the best book I've ever read, and I can't wait to put it into action."

WAYNE G. MILLER, associate vice-president, business development and consulting, SunLife

STRATEGY
TO
ACTION

Run Your Business
Without It Running You

STRATEGY TO ACTION

KEITA DEMMING,PhD

Cataloguing in publication information is available from Library and Archives Canada.

ISBN 978-1-77458-270-1 (paperback)
ISBN 978-1-77458-271-8 (ebook)

Page Two
pagetwo.com

Edited by Sarah Brohman
Copyedited by David Marsh
Cover design by Jennifer Lum
Interior design by Setareh Ashrafologhalai

Interior illustrations by
Setareh Ashrafologhalai and Jeffrey Winocur

keitademming.com

To my late grandmother Hannah,
who inspired me to be an educator.

To my parents, Richard and Dennise
Demming, who have always supported me
and inspired me to be a lifelong learner.

To my friend and mentor Norm Trainor,
who founded The Covenant Group and has
helped me turn my avocation into a vocation.

To my wife, Shauna, who insisted that
I make the time and space to write this book.

To my son, Oliver, who at a tender
age has taught me things
I did not know I needed to learn.

CONTENTS

1

THE GAP BETWEEN STRATEGY AND TACTICS

"Without strategy, execution is aimless.
Without execution, strategy is useless."
MORRIS CHANG

THERE WAS once a group of mice who lived in constant fear of the cat in the house. One clever mouse suggested they put a bell around the cat's neck so they could hear it coming. The other mice thought this was a great idea until one wise mouse asked, "But who is going to put the bell on the cat's neck?" The mice had a winning strategy, but they had not considered the tactics needed to achieve their goal.

Welcome to the gap between strategy and tactics.

In my role as an advisor and coach at The Covenant Group, I meet "mice" all the time. A company leader or someone on their team appears to have a brilliant strategy to solve a pressing problem or achieve a desired business goal, but they have not considered how they are going to implement that strategy. Too many dreams die because people use poor metaphors and frameworks when they try to think strategically about how to live their lives and accomplish their business goals. At the same time they can overcomplicate strategy and tactics and get hopelessly tangled up in competing obligations. The business runs them instead of them running the business.

Strategy is not a definitive plan that promises, or even delivers, certain results. Instead, I encourage you to think of strategy as an ongoing conversation, an ongoing inquiry into what you want and where you are going. Strategy is a hypothesis about what you need to do to get somewhere or achieve something. Tactics are how you test that hypothesis. Strategy is abstract. Tactics are concrete. But most importantly, when you align your strategy with your tactics effectively, you make it possible to shape the future and make your dreams a reality.

At The Covenant Group, we've learned through working with our clients that if they want to change their future, the first step is for them to ask better questions about what they want their future to look like. Better questions invite better conversations that can lead to a better alignment between strategy and tactics. In short, better conversations make for better business.

In the pages to come, I will introduce you to our Strategy Quadrant tool, an effective way for you to have conversations about strategy—with yourself, with your inner circle, and with the people you serve. The Strategy Quadrant teaches you how to focus on those things that are strategic and tactical, while encouraging you to consider the consequences for both the short and long term. The further out you plan, the more uncertainty you embrace. You will learn how to use the Strategy Quadrant to test your strategy, with an eye on both the short and long term, so that you can move from strategy to action.

The Strategy Quadrant tool is a product of my work as a former academic-turned-educator and coach combined with practical experience and feedback from the clients of The Covenant Group. Over 35,000 entrepreneurs have gone through our programs in the last twenty-five years, and I have seen first-hand how this tool has transformed the lives of our clients. Their experiences have informed the writing of this book and its stories. For reasons of confidentiality, I have used a mix of composite characters and pseudonyms in some of the case studies, alongside real-life case stories.

The examples I share in this book focus on people who want to build a business, grow an existing business, or help someone else build a business. Even though the ideas and advice in this book can apply equally to both life and business, my mission is to help people become better businesspeople, and to become better people in business. I believe that you cannot separate the two. To that end, this book is intended for people who embrace the spirit of entrepreneurship and who want to make a difference in this world.

You will learn from a personal trainer who took his business from $50,000 a year to just shy of a million dollars by asking better questions about the future. As he would say, he was able to help more people live in a body they love. We will also share the story of a Canadian wine company that is embracing uncertainty as part of its strategy and as a result is becoming one of the best wineries in the world. You will learn about Nassor, who struggled in his role as owner and CEO and realized he needed to demote himself to head of marketing if he was going to grow the company. You will learn about Haesun, who escaped the "tyranny of the urgent"—the habit of spending our time on those things that are urgent, immediate, or pressing instead of prioritizing actions based on relative importance—and went on to publish her first book because she was able to redesign the things she did in the short term.

So, if you are an entrepreneur or busy professional who finds yourself bogged down in the tyranny of the urgent, this book is for you. If you are struggling to understand what is meant by strategy and tactics, this book is for you. If you want to develop an action plan that helps you implement your desired future, this book is for you.

It's my hope that after reading this book you will go into the world and turn your dreams into reality. But at the very least, you should be able to clearly answer this important question: How do I radically serve my desired future? Unfortunately, people often sabotage the future by neglecting or even avoiding thinking about what kind of future they do want. They may

Think of strategy as an ongoing conversation, an ongoing inquiry about what you want and where you are going.

try to play the long game, but when life is coming at them fast, with bills to pay and clients to serve, they feel like they are on a hamster wheel and too busy to be thinking about the future.

Some people describe their life as an adventure. Others describe it as a mission, a pursuit, or a journey. But no matter how you describe your life, these words are all synonyms for a quest for a better future. To increase your odds of succeeding, you need to first ask the right questions within meaningful conversations and view each stage of your journey as a new question. This takes time and thinking and starts with an immediate investment in the future.

You might believe you don't have time to think about or play the long game, but you do. With the help of the Strategy Quadrant tool, you can learn how to integrate the future you desire with the habits, routines, and actions you take today. You will not only understand why it is important to align your strategies and tactics, but also be able to build the roadmap that will take you there. But most of all, you will learn how to move from strategy to action so you can take your business to the next level.

So, let's get started! I'll show you how a simple thought framework can help you make the most of your strategy and close the gap between it and the tactics you need to reach your goals.

In the next chapter I'll talk about how we've been miseducated about the purpose of strategy as some kind of exact science that guarantees the perfect outcome.

REFLECTION POINTS

- To accomplish your business goals, think more about how you can close the gap between your strategy and your tactics.

- Strategy is a hypothesis and tactics are how you test that hypothesis.

- Think of strategy as an ongoing conversation.

- Better conversations make for better business.

As we learn from readers like you, we will continue to develop tools and resources to help you move from strategy to action. To access this supplementary material, please visit keitademming.com or scan the QR code below.

2

THE MISEDUCATION OF MANAGEMENT

"Uncertainty is the only certainty
there is, and knowing how to live with
insecurity is the only security."

JOHN ALLEN PAULOS

THERE ARE events in history that change the way we see the world. One such day was September 16, 1992, also known as Black Wednesday, when financier George Soros broke the Bank of England. Central bankers in Europe were in the midst of creating a single currency, the Euro. But one big question remained: Would Great Britain join the Euro club?

At the time, George Soros and his team managed one of the largest hedge funds in the world. They made a bet that Great Britain would not adopt the Euro and as a result the price of the pound would fall. Soros and his team shorted the British pound sterling, which meant that if the value of the currency dropped, they would make money. At the time, Soros's hedge fund, Quantum Capital, was valued at five billion dollars. Soros and his hedge fund team agreed to bet three times Quantum's fund, or fifteen billion dollars. If they were right, they could bankrupt the Bank of England, a move that would send shock waves through the European financial system. The events that unfolded were historic. George Soros and his team shorted the Bank of England and won. When all was said and done, British taxpayers lost $3.8 billion. And in one day, Soros and his team made, by some estimates, one billion dollars.

Make no mistake, this is yet another story of the rich getting richer. There are also ethical questions to consider. Not to mention the incredibly risky and unrecommended move of shorting stocks. If Great Britain had adopted the Euro, Soros would have had to pay the Bank of England an outrageous amount of money. The stakes here were as high as they could be, yet Soros and his team accounted for the soft side of the dynamic by paying attention to the egos and emotions of the key decision makers.

Over the years I have read many accounts of these events, but one from Christian Madsbjerg's book *Sensemaking: The Power of the Humanities in the Age of the Algorithm* stands out the most for me. What makes Madsbjerg's account so distinctive is his analysis of how Soros and his team knew to make that bet when only a few made the same or a similar move. They did not rely solely on financial and economic models. Instead, Soros's analysts realized that the personal dynamics between the president of the German central bank, Helmut Schlesinger, and the British finance minister, Norman Lamont, would determine the outcome of these events. The president and the finance minister were increasingly antagonistic to one another and the chances of them coming to an agreement were small.

In their final decision, Soros and his team considered data based on the complexity of human emotions: How did these two decision makers feel about each other and the situation? And how would their animosity affect the outcome of Britain's decision on the Euro? In the end, what the Soros team realized is that human beings are complex, and the team needed to account for the unpredictability that people bring to the way they make decisions. Soros made the bet of a lifetime fully acknowledging that despite what the data and models predicted, the fate of the Euro would be defined by two fallible human beings. (I would like to have been in the room when that conversation was taking place.)

The Inconvenient Reality

The often unarticulated dilemma around strategy creation is that no matter what decision you make, there is no way to guarantee the outcome. We behave as if the world is certain and we can know the answer(s) in advance, but our actions and beliefs often contradict the way the world unfolds.

One example of a similar dilemma is the way we, at least in North America, think and talk about death. Religious beliefs aside, few of us would disagree that death is inevitable. Yet so often we behave as if it is not. One Gallup poll estimated that 54 percent of North Americans do not have a will. Yet 100 percent of them are going to die. Just as we avoid conversations related to death and dying, when it comes to business strategy, leaders and management tend to ignore how uncertain and complex the world is.

In his now classic publications, *The Rise and Fall of Strategic Planning* (1994) and *Tracking Strategies: Towards a General Theory of Strategy Formation* (2007), Henry Mintzberg introduces the idea of emergent strategy. Mintzberg studied hundreds of strategies implemented by organizations. In his research, he discovered that few, if any, business strategy plans ever unfold as intended.

Managers and leaders tend to react to this unpredictability by adopting one of two approaches:

1　They assume and act "as if" they can predict how things will unfold.

2　They argue that planning does not make sense because they cannot predict how the world will unfold.

This discomfort of acting in a world of unknowing is at the heart of why strategy is often done so poorly. And today's business strategies are also influenced by old management thinking, inheriting ideas from an era that was predominated by factory work. That era produced a form of thinking called scientific management, not without its shortcomings, which brought great success at the time and still permeates many aspects of management thinking. Peter Drucker once stated that scientific management "may well be the most powerful as well as the most lasting contribution America has made to Western thought since the Federalist Papers." Consequently, many of us have been miseducated when it comes to creating and thinking about strategy.

For years many business leaders have operated "as if" the workplace is like a machine. My brother is a mechanic and I find it interesting to compare our lines of work. As a mechanic, he is called on to repair cars. He can usually pinpoint a malfunctioning part such as a broken hose. He orders the part, replaces it, and his job is done, at least until another part breaks. If, however, you stumble upon a group of people who aren't getting along, there is no repair shop to take them to. We cannot identify a part, replace it, and call it a day. What more often happens is that we resolve one issue and something else emerges. We address that challenge, and a new dynamic appears.

Many leaders and businesspeople behave as if a mechanical approach will work with human systems. We do this, we get that result. We send the car to be repaired and it will be perfectly fine. I refer to this as the "organization as a machine" metaphor and it is pervasive in how many leaders think and talk about the workplace. Scientific management treats the workplace like the car that needs to be fixed, when it is more dynamic and fluid and full of human behaviour that isn't always predictable.

It's time for new thinking that embraces learning, uncertainty, and adaptability.

It's time for new thinking that embraces learning, uncertainty, and adaptability. The paradigm has changed. Today's world is vastly more complex and increasingly geared toward the knowledge worker. Instead of an "if this, then that" kind of thinking, what if you adopted an approach of "if this, then maybe"? The irony is that we have already bought into this idea at some level. You'll find it living in well-known quotations such as Robert Burns's "the best-laid plans of mice and men often go awry," or "everyone has a plan until they get hit," which is often attributed to Mike Tyson but has a much longer history. These proverbial sayings suggest that we already know the world is tremendously uncertain.

However, often what we see in the world are company leaders clinging to an illusion of predictability and certainty, mostly because it gives them comfort. That comfort, however, is an illusion. Certainty can exist only when all variables and risks are known. We need to stop behaving "as if" the world is predictable. Too many strategy plans and models behave "as if" they exist in a world where all variables are known. In an increasingly uncertain world, I want to help you change your thinking about strategy and tactics so that it matches this inconvenient reality.

Changing the Conversation

What business leaders and management need most today is an approach to strategy that helps reduce risk and strikes a balance between short-term needs and long-term strategic goals. One that considers that organizations and workplaces are not objective, reducible spaces with universal truths. Organizations are complex human arrangements where people play games, seek to increase their influence, and strive for recognition and power. This is what Soros and his team under-stood when they made their billion-dollar bet on the British pound. They wagered that the decision would come down to two people with an emotional history and bruised egos.

Here is a simple thought experiment that reflects this: Assume you and three friends are having a great conversation. Now suppose for some reason one of those friends leaves the conversation midstream and is replaced by another, unknown person. Will the conversation still maintain the same level of energy, insight, and flow? This seems awkward, doesn't it? The new conversation partner will need context for your con-versation. They will bring a different perspective and sense of humour. They might be confused or feel left out and that might affect what they contribute. When you replace someone in an organization, you are essentially replacing a conversa-tion partner.

In my work and research, I find it helpful to think of orga-nizations as a conversation. And yet, the old ideas related to scientific management are hard to dislodge because people are not always aware that they hold an "if this, then that" kind of mental model. When you think about an organization as a conversation, you can quickly see how it influences the condi-tions of possibility. You can, for example, ask more interesting questions like:

- Who is contributing to the conversation and, consequently, the decisions?

- Who is not in the conversation and should be?

- What questions and conversations do you need to improve the conditions of possibility?

- Which conversations put you in a better position to achieve your desired future?

What we do not realize is that the conversation is the action. When we see organizations as a conversation, we begin to see how much more compatible the approach is with an "if this, then maybe" view of the world.

CHANGING YOUR thinking about how you view your business is never easy. So, at the end of this chapter, the question I most want you to consider is: What would be different if you approached the world with an "if this, then maybe" mindset? With this new way of thinking you might also be able to see that solving problems isn't always that simple.

REFLECTION POINTS

- The world is complex and there is no way to guarantee your strategy will work. Few, if any, strategies ever unfold as intended.

- Your strategy should take an approach that embraces learning, uncertainty, and adaptability.

- Most leaders could benefit from an "if this, then maybe" way of viewing the world, in contrast to the dominant "if this, then that" approach.

- Think of your organization like a relationship and not like a machine.

TRY THIS:

1   As you move through the world, notice where you see the "organization as a machine" metaphor evoked.

2   The next time you are in a conversation that is focused on the short term, try to shift the focus of the conversation to the long term where it's appropriate. You can do this by asking a time-related question like, How would this decision impact us in ten years?

3

WHAT KIND OF PROBLEM(S) ARE YOU CONFRONTING?

"We fail more often because we solve the
wrong problem than because we get
the wrong solution to the right problem."

RUSSELL L. ACKOFF

O N JULY 11, 1810, Australian explorer Frederick Hasselborough stumbled upon a remote island located between Australia and Antarctica that he named Macquarie Island. The island was inhabited by seals and penguins, animals that were hunted for their oils. Over time, Macquarie Island became a popular destination for hunters and with them came rats from their ships. With no natural predators on the island, the rats thrived. To cull the burgeoning rodent population, the hunters introduced cats to the island, and then rabbits to provide themselves with a food source. (I am not a big fan of cats, yet I have somehow managed to tell two stories about cats in this book.)

Unfortunately, these invasive animals created havoc for the island's fragile ecosystem. The cats devastated the bird populations so much that from 1985 to 2000 efforts were undertaken to eliminate the feline population. Once the cats were removed, the rabbit and rat populations exploded. The rabbits ate so much vegetation that they increased the erosion of the landscape, which resulted in landslides. Efforts were then made to eliminate the rat and rabbit populations and finally, in 2012, island was announced to be free of cats, rats, and rabbits. Curiously, the island is still plagued by many invasive birds introduced over the years.

This story is often told as a cautionary tale of unintended consequences. But there's a different outcome I want to emphasize. The first assumption that was made was that this was a simple problem. Consequently, the strategy for addressing it was accordingly simple. The second assumption was that the problem was solvable. Before you can even begin to define your strategy, you need to ask, What kind of problem(s) are we confronting?

What's Your Problem?

In his book *The Wisdom of Crowds*, James Surowiecki points out that there are three kinds of problems:

- Cognitive: problems that can be resolved through logic and reasoning.

- Coordination: problems of getting resources to the same time and place.

- Collaboration: problems of getting people to genuinely work together.

Like many, I have so often struggled to get people to collaborate. The times when it has worked well have been when we all believed in the large reason we were working together—what my friend and author David Burkus would call the "cause worth fighting for." What I had not realized was that I was approaching collaboration as a simple problem. In reading Surowiecki's distinctions of the various types of problems, it struck me that collaboration is a complex problem, yet we often approach it "as if" it is a simple or complicated problem. But how do you differentiate between a simple, complicated, or complex problem?

When I was working at the University of Waterloo, I had the great fortune to work alongside the late Brenda Zimmerman, who was an incredible academic and thinker. She used an insightful metaphor in making a distinction between simple, complicated, and complex problems. Zimmerman described simple problems as being like baking a cake, where cause and effect are closely linked in time. If you follow a recipe, you can be fairly certain that the outcome will be close to the intended one. Even someone with little experience can follow a recipe for baking a cake and get reliable results.

With complicated problems, cause and effect are often separated by time. You can think of complicated problems as similar to planning a large outdoor festival or even launching a rocket. Although complicated problems often follow a particular formula, they usually require high levels of expertise and a considerable amount of planning. But with enough time, resources, planning, and expertise, the results can be reliably attainable and repeatable.

Complex problems are different in that they are more like growing a garden or raising children. When you plant seeds in a garden you never know if they will bear fruit or if a rabbit will eat your vegetables. Similarly, when it comes to raising children, one thing is for certain: children are not passive, and the process is dynamic. As adults attempt new parenting strategies, children tend to change their responses. As the children change their responses, parents in turn try new strategies and approaches or emergent practices. There are no tried-and-true formulas for raising children. (When I first learned this, I was childless. Now that I have a child, the term "complex problem" takes on an entirely new meaning.)

In my experience, too many people approach their problems "as if " they are simple when they might be complicated. Too few take the time to figure out what type of problem they are facing. As a result, their strategy going into the problem is rarely fit for purpose. For example, introducing cats to take care of the rats on Macquarie Island assumed that both the problem and the solution were simple. Complex problems are dynamic and so it's often difficult to build a business that solves them consistently. The challenge is that all organizations have complex problems within them.

SIMPLE PROBLEMS	COMPLICATED PROBLEMS	COMPLEX PROBLEMS
Repeatable, predictable, and quantifiable	Requires expertise and resources	Requires emergent practices
Example: sending an invoice	Example: migrating to a new Customer Relationship Management system	Example: team building

Let's return to the complicated problem of launching a rocket. The technical aspects of launching a rocket can be addressed by engineers and resolved with the right resources and expertise. The challenge is that teams involve autonomous agents we call people. And finding a way for people to work together is inherently a complex problem. A good example can be found in Amy Edmondson's book *Teaming: How Organizations Learn, Innovate, and Compete in the Knowledge Economy*.

In her book, Edmondson tells the story of the Columbia space shuttle disaster, in which seven astronauts perished as the shuttle returned from orbit. The core of the story revolved around video footage of the launch. Engineer Rodney Rocha observed debris falling off the shuttle and striking the left wing of the shuttle. This observation concerned Rocha and he requested satellite images from his senior manager, which also required the involvement of the US Department of

Defense. When his request was denied, Rocha sent an email to engineer colleagues and also voiced his concerns at a management meeting. But in NASA's culture, engineers were not supposed to email higher-ups, and had Rocha continued to voice his concerns, it may have been career-limiting for him. Later investigations concluded that the cause of the accident was a briefcase-sized object that damaged the shuttle's wing.

Although this is an extreme case of ineffective teamwork, it shows how working in teams is a complex problem, while the engineering involved in launching a rocket is a complicated problem. The Columbia space shuttle engineers had valid concerns and were afraid to speak up; they did not enjoy "psychological safety." Other members of the team spotted the problem but did not speak up.

My dad, who is also an engineer, always says that "the engineering is easy, it's the people and politics that are hard." Only an engineer would say the engineering was easy! I would say the engineering is complicated; it's the people and politics that make it complex. Rarely do we give complex problems the time and space they need.

Some years ago, a company reached out to me to do team-building with them. They wanted me to do it in a single day and expected that their team would be instantly transformed by the experience. They saw me as the car mechanic who could repair the team in one visit. But team-building is a complex problem because there is no simple formula you can apply to magically create high-performing teams.

Teams involve dynamics between flawed humans who, unlike the parts of a car, come with relationship histories, emotions, and personalities. High-performing teams require ongoing work. It is here that the distinctions between simple, complicated, and complex problems can become a competitive advantage. If leaders can recognize that they are facing a complex problem, they can then design approaches to address complex problems.

Take the company that wanted a one-day team-building session. The person who wanted to hire me was competing against a similar team in her department and wanted to create a culture that outperformed the other team. Six months after she hired another consultant, she saw that nothing had changed in her team's performance. So, she approached me again after I had turned her down the first time. This time we worked out an eighteen-month plan during which we would teach her team sales effectiveness and develop a performance measurement system to ensure her team was reaching its targets. We used a combination of training and coaching to help her transform her culture. Fourteen months later, her team was outselling the rival team by a three-to-one margin and her team morale was high.

During that process, she realized a simple one-day training session was not going to solve a complex problem. What she needed was an ongoing approach that could help her build a culture over time. As you move through this book, whenever you think about your strategy, start by asking, What kind of problem am I facing? If it is a simple problem, then you know you can use a recipe. If it is a complicated problem, then you know you need to source expertise and spend time working out the details. If it is a complex problem, you need to treat it as fluid or emergent.

One of the fundamental lessons of working within a complex world, however, is that we cannot manage or avoid complexity, we can only tame it. There are no solutions to complexity, only antidotes. For example, when the client I mentioned above finally got her team to perform well, we had to adjust the compensation model. In the previous structure, only the lead person received a commission, even though it took the team to work on the sale. People expressed that it was unfair that they were not receiving a commission when they were obviously part of that team. As we tamed one challenge, another one emerged. This dynamic is often swept under the rug and, eventually, that results in a lumpy rug. At The Covenant Group, we often say the antidote to complexity is inquiry: asking questions and listening. But having a conversation is not enough—you need to understand how to frame that conversation so you can address it over the long term.

Following the Grape

Years ago, my wife and I visited what has become our favourite winery, Pearl Morissette in Jordan, Ontario. We followed a gravel road to a large barn and after we figured out where the entrance was, we finally joined the group for our scheduled tasting tour. During the tour we were given the option to select four wines for tasting. Since I am not typically a white wine drinker, I chose four different reds. My wife got two whites and two reds. After tasting the wines, my wife suggested I try the whites she had selected. To my surprise, I enjoyed each one. It was the first time that I had enjoyed a white wine. Then I got curious: What made these wines so different? Our guide explained that at Pearl Morissette they "follow the grape."

Most companies mass-produce their wine and so their goal is quantity and consistency. They try to create the same taste year over year so that each time you choose one of their bottles, you know exactly what it is going to taste like. Instead, Pearl Morissette competes on quality by following what the grape tells them. Managing partner François Morissette does not consider himself a winemaker. "He prefers the term vigneron, a French word without an English equivalent, referring to a person who guides the grapes along their journey from vine to bottle," said a 2018 article in the *New York Times*. "Indeed, shepherding is how Mr. Morissette sees his job, not so much manufacturing wine as helping the grapes realize their destiny."

Although other producers may try to force the grape to fit some predetermined idea of what the wine should taste like, in its "follow the grape" approach, Morissette enters into a conversation with the grape by first understanding the problems it may have experienced during its growing season. At the start of the year the team at Pearl Morissette looks at the weather conditions and asks questions like, Did it rain more than usual or was it dry? Was it a cold or warm year? All those climatic conditions make a difference to how the grapes grow and how they will taste. Only after the team has answered those questions will they know how to make the wine. They start the conversation with the wine by asking questions, and each season they develop a sub-strategy for how they will make wine for that season.

Most winemakers look at their work as if it were a simple process—use this recipe and adjust it so the wine tastes the same every year. But Pearl Morissette sees winemaking as complex. They have no interest in trying to force their wines to taste the same each year. Instead, each year they choose to follow the grape and produce a great wine. This decision also means they cannot scale in the way other winemakers can because their model creates a low supply of high-quality wines. Yet, because they produce such great wines, the demand for their product is always high, so the business model works.

The owner-operators of Pearl Morissette believe they can win with a focus on producing high-quality wines rather than forcing simplicity onto a complex process. They have a conversation with the grape, which has the effect of stimulating a conversation about the final result of their winemaking. After

Conversations that improve the conditions of possibility create tremendous value.

all, the antidote to complexity is asking questions and listening to the answers. Conversations that improve the conditions of possibility create tremendous value.

The uncomfortable truth is that many business leaders want to know exactly how their strategies will unfold. Certainty is comforting. Uncertainty and complexity are scary and risky. When you behave as if the world is certain, you can fall victim to an illusion of certainty. And more importantly, when you act as if the world is certain, you undermine your strategy. So how then do you approach complexity? To do so requires that you:

1 Name it to tame it: identify complex problems and understand that you cannot avoid complexity, you can only tame it.

2 Acknowledge that the antidote to complexity is inquiry: asking questions and listening.

3 Accept that formulating strategy is an ongoing conversation. Whatever strategy you have today should be thought of as a temporary holding position. When the assumptions about your strategy change, you need to change your strategy.

I once shared the Pearl Morissette story at a workshop and a client pointed out that as climate change continues to be a challenge, she thought traditional winemakers would struggle to grow the grapes that would provide a consistent taste. From her perspective, Pearl Morissette was building a more resilient, future-proof organization that could withstand the changing climate.

The "follow the grape" approach is so different from the dominant one that it can sometimes be hard to get buy-in from senior leaders to adopt this more flexible and responsive approach. It all starts with having a conversation with your team, asking questions, listening, and absorbing.

NOW THAT you understand that strategy is not a certain science and how important it is for you to determine what kind of problem you want to solve with your strategy, you are almost ready to have a better conversation using the tool of the Strategy Quadrant. At The Covenant Group, we have found that the most helpful way to think about and implement strategy is by adopting the mindsets of an Eagle and a Wolf. In the next chapter, we explore how those mindsets operate within a company and how balancing their influences contributes to your conversation about strategy and leads to your desired future.

REFLECTION POINTS

- Determine if you are dealing with a simple, complicated, or complex problem when formulating your strategy.

- Complex problems benefit from a "follow the grape" solution-based approach.

- The antidote to complexity is inquiry and conversation.

TRY THIS:

As you move through the world, identify a simple problem, a complicated problem, and a complex problem. Take the time to write them down and pay attention to how people try to address these problems.

4

THE EAGLE AND THE WOLF

"Great vision without great people is irrelevant."

JIM COLLINS

AM OFTEN asked why we use the analogy of the Eagle and Wolf in the Strategy Quadrant tool. A key education principle we use in the design of our programs is to build on what our clients already know. When I describe the Eagle and Wolf mindsets through the lens of the Strategy Quadrant, this metaphor lands with clients almost universally and is immediately clear.

When you are carving out strategy, there are times when you need to see the big picture, and then there are times when you should be focused on implementation on the ground. The Strategy Quadrant uses the Eagle and Wolf mindsets to help you conceptualize this. Think of the Eagle mindset as those things related to strategy, and your Wolf activities as things that focus on execution and implementation—in other words, tactical steps. We call the capacity to move between these mindsets "shapeshifting." This capacity to shapeshift between the two ways of thinking and operating is something you need to embrace in thinking about, understanding, and applying the Strategy Quadrant to your business.

To realize your desired future, you need both strategy and tactics. If you want your business to make an impact and achieve something meaningful in the world, you will need to be both strategic and tactical. The challenge is that many people are often stronger in one mindset or the other. So, as you build out your plan to realize your desired future, you will also need to make sure you have the right combination of Eagle- and Wolf-type thinking and thinkers in your business.

See Like the Eagle

Eagles are tremendous hunters. In many cultures, they represent strength, wisdom, knowledge, resilience, and endurance. Their tremendous vision means they can see up to eight times better than humans and can spot small prey from nearly three miles away. To survive, they need to decide where they are going to hunt and must be discerning about how they will expend energy. For eagles, the question is simple: Where are they most likely to find food? If they do not choose well, they will starve. Understanding strategy is about understanding where you are most likely to succeed. When you step into the Eagle mindset, you are deciding how you will spend resources, time, and energy so you can thrive and win.

In the Eagle mindset, you focus on two objectives:

1 Taking the bird's-eye view and getting clear on where you want to be five or even ten years from now.

2 Clarifying where you are going to play to win.

Roger Martin, professor emeritus at the Rotman School of Management at the University of Toronto, is one of the leading thinkers on strategy. He defines strategy as "an integrative set of choices that positions you on a playing field of your choice in a way that you win." Strategy done well is about developing guidelines that continually guide you to make choices that help you realize your desired future.

The common downfall in most approaches to strategy is that people tend to view strategy as a plan and not a planning process. I never want you to be part of a strategy planning process that simply sits on a shelf and has zero impact on the choices you make. Your strategy should inform and frame the choices you make every day. And that's where the wolves come in.

Change Course Like the Wolf

I used to teach design and systems thinking to young adults. One video I would use in my workshops was called "How Wolves Change Rivers." It demonstrated what happened when a small group of wolves was reintroduced to Yellowstone National Park. Prior to their reintroduction, wolves were absent from the park because of overhunting. Since there were no wolves to hunt large prey, the deer population exploded and grazed away most of the vegetation. Since there was no vegetation, there was nothing to hold the soil in place. This caused significant erosion and much of the park was left barren.

Once the wolves were reintroduced, the deer started avoiding the open areas where the wolves could easily hunt them. The presence of the wolves changed the behaviour of the deer, and the areas they had frequented began to regenerate. As the vegetation slowly returned, so did other wildlife. What is most remarkable is that the river began to change course as well. As the vegetation returned, the banks of the river became more stable, which altered the course of the river overall. Reintroducing this small group of wolves into the park completely changed the geography and ecology of the landscape.

How does all this apply to the integration of strategy and implementation?

One client to whom I introduced this way of thinking told me, "You just gave me permission to go and hire wolves." It is

People are
more concerned
about status
and compensation
than impact and
influence.

true. The team you create is critical to your success. Regardless of what you are trying to accomplish, you need to foster a strong team that can execute your strategy. The wolves on your team are the people on the ground who execute the tactics. One of the phrases I use in my coaching is that businesses should have "no weak wolves." This phrase is inspired by a quotation from Rudyard Kipling's *The Jungle Book*: "For the strength of the pack is the wolf, and the strength of the wolf is the pack." If you are going to have an impact on the people you serve, you need a team that can change the course of rivers.

Risk and Reward

Whatever your strategy, your planning process begins with a vision of the future you desire. Executing that plan will depend on whether you have the right mix of Eagle and Wolf mindsets on your team. Companies that are full of people who are risk averse do not have Eagles and Wolves. Eagles and Wolves are not afraid of taking risk. They are not afraid to speak up. Having this mindset in your team is important because who you enlist in your strategy is part of the strategy itself.

In chapter 2, I introduced the story of George Soros, the man who broke the Bank of England. Soros and his team understood that despite what the models said, it was past conversations between two men that would be the determining factor in the question of whether England would adopt the Euro. Soros and his team were engaged in an ongoing conversation about the risks and rewards they were confronting. They had a hypothesis about what would happen. There was no way to test it, but they knew if they were right, they would win big. They were primarily concerned with the questions, How are we going to play to win? How are we going to beat the

Bank of England? These were big strategic questions shrouded in risk and uncertainty. Soros had a team of Eagles and Wolves. When it was time to make the call, they were all ready to make the calculated decision. Their continuous assessment of risk and reward is what led them to such great success.

When you engage in true strategy, it won't feel entirely comfortable. You should be slightly nervous. You should have tossed around a number of scenarios, and you should believe your approach gives you the best chance of winning in uncertain circumstances.

Gerd Gigerenzer is the author of *Risk Savvy: How to Make Good Decisions*. In his book he dedicates an entire chapter to what he calls "defensive decision making." Gigerenzer argues that investors often focus on avoiding short-term loss instead of focusing on more lucrative long-term investments. Judges make conservative decisions and rely on precedence and established rules instead of looking at the context or circumstances of the case. His main point is that in a wide array of professions, people avoid making mistakes and being held accountable for negative outcomes. As a consequence, people make less savvy decisions instead of taking calculated risks.

In some company cultures, people in leadership positions do everything they can to avoid making mistakes. In these companies, people are more concerned about status and compensation than impact and influence. These folks are guided by the questions, How do I not lose my job? How do I not make a mistake?

These companies are stacked with people who are simply trying to get noticed enough that they get a promotion and a raise. Their goal is to not get fired before they have paid off their mortgage or are ready to retire. These conditions produce people who are risk averse, which makes their companies risk averse. In the end, when you play to avoid losing, paradoxically you increase risk. When you go along to get along, you do not put yourself and your company in a position to win. Companies filled with risk-averse people stifle change and innovation.

It is imperative that you and your team understand what it means to develop strategies under conditions of uncertainty and risk. You can have certainty only if you know all the risks and variables and that your assumptions are completely accurate. That is never the case because we live in a world of incomplete information or unknowns. Where you want to get to is to feel confident that you and your team have made a solid decision in the face of risk and uncertainty. And getting to confident takes, you guessed it, a conversation with yourself and your team.

Conversation Makes You Resilient

Earlier I introduced the idea that organizations are not machines but conversations. And those conversations are often full of stories and metaphors that allow us to share different perspectives. We accomplish nothing in life without conversation—it is where true change begins. When you view your world as a machine that is stable and predictable, and not as emergent and fluid like a conversation, you might be making yourself less resilient in an increasingly complex world.

More than a decade ago, I worked with a client organization on a project that turned out to be an abysmal failure, or at least I thought so. At the time, I was excited because I had just landed my first major client. It was exactly the kind of work I wanted to be doing. When my services were terminated, I was left scratching my head and asking myself two questions: What could I have done differently? Where did it all go wrong?

A few years later I ran into Dora, who was one of the most talented people at the organization and someone I really enjoyed working with. When she told me that I had completely transformed how she thought about organizations, I was surprised and the only response I could muster up was to ask her to tell me how. She told me, "I have never forgotten your description of organizations as conversations and not machines." She explained that understanding organizations as conversations made her pay close attention to the language she uses with her team. She now pays attention to who speaks first, how things are framed, and how her comments or questions influence future conversations and eventually the actions of those on her team.

"Forgive me Dora," I said, "but that was one of my worst consulting experiences and I am surprised you got so much out of it." What Dora told me next was an eye-opener. She told me that "the challenge was that the CEO always saw the organization as a machine. It's why the two of you never worked well together, and ultimately why I left. Once I started working at another organization, I could see how understanding organizations as conversations could unleash the latent potential within them."

Workplaces are intense social spaces full of things like teaming, collaboration, and innovation. They are also full of things like paradoxes, game-playing, and alliance-building. Business leaders and managers should treat them as such. Many managers have been taught to find the right answer, to look for silver bullets, or the one thing that will make the company more effective or efficient. These can be successful approaches, but a more effective way of going about this is to acknowledge that the decisions you make in your workplace are based on your interpretations of the world.

We make decisions based on the conversations we have or want to have, and those that we don't have. We need better conversations with ourselves, with people in our inner circle, and with the industry and people we seek to serve. And better conversations often begin with good questions.

A Sound Strategy Seeks Confidence

When I spoke to Svetlana Atcheva, brand ambassador for Pearl Morissette, she explained that the company's ambition is to make one of the best wines in the world. Their approach to making wine is a traditional, old-world one—the follow-the-grape approach—whereas most other winemakers prefer the factory model. Of course, it would be easier for the company to be profitable if they took the factory approach. But if they did, their chances of producing a wine that could be considered one of the best in the world would be lowered dramatically.

Svetlana and her team are clear on who they are and where they are going, and that clarity of vision and mission helps them make good choices. They are able to have better conversations about strategy because they are clear about their desired future.

Pearl Morissette's strategic hypothesis is that if they make the best wine possible, they can make a Canadian wine one of the best in the world. And their business strategy is to relentlessly commit to the highest-quality product and not what the market is demanding. That makes them disruptors in the wine world. And although Pearl Morissette is not certain their strategy will work, they are confident that it will. Case in point: their business strategy helped them weather the disruption of the pandemic. When the pandemic hit, Pearl Morissette had already cultivated direct relationships with their customers and were set up for online sales, unlike most other wineries in Canada, which sold to distributors, who sold to the end client.

This distinction between being certain your strategy will work and having confidence in your strategy is the line you must walk up to. A sound strategy seeks confidence. Seeking certainty is a dead end because there is no such thing. When you are truly strategic, it should feel a little uncertain. I have seen countless scenarios where a leader chooses not to move forward with a bold and progressive strategy because they could not guarantee success. The big takeaway here is that when people are clear about their future direction, they can have better conversations about how they will realize that future.

Metaphors Make a Difference

Metaphors frame the way we see the world and it is important that you use the right ones as you align strategies and tactics. When you change the metaphor you use, you also change the kinds of questions you ask and the strategies you use.

Many years ago, I was working with an ambitious entrepreneur. Chad was the founder of a very exciting start-up. The company was growing quickly, but Chad and his team were struggling with the execution of their business strategies. Each time we met, Chad would describe his company as a family. He would say, "We all love each other and get along well, yet something is not working." I explained to him, "Metaphors play a very important role in the kinds of questions we ask and the way we think about our organizations. You consistently describe your company as a family—what would be different about your company if you thought of it as a team?"

Almost surprising himself, he responded, "Some of the people in the company would not be here." That insight caught him off guard. Until then, Chad had never considered

We make decisions
based on the
conversations we
have or want to have,
and those that we
don't have.

replacing some of his family members. After all, they were exactly that: family. The metaphor of the family was blocking him from the difficult decisions he needed to make. When he thought of his company as a family, it meant that he was accepting mediocre work.

Initially, Chad's conversation with himself was guided by a specific metaphor. But when Chad started thinking about his company as a team rather than a family, he began to see it in a new way. He changed his metaphor, which changed the way in which he asked questions about his company. That simple change of lens helped him find new answers to the problems the company was struggling with.

After our conversation, Chad arranged performance reviews and generous exit packages for the individuals he realized were not cut out to be a part of the company's journey. He began to hire people who were better suited to the roles. These were difficult decisions for Chad and it was a challenging time for the company overall. But six months later, Chad told me that although this transition was a difficult time, he was much better off once he committed to building a team rather than a family.

AS YOU learn to work with the Strategy Quadrant and its principles in the following chapters, you will see how its primary purpose is to help you continually make choices that serve your desired future, whether that is transitioning your business to your heirs, gaining more market share, or even running your first marathon. Most of all, it can help you have a better conversation about strategy so you arrive at that place of confidence and make decisions that set you up for success.

REFLECTION POINTS

- The ability to shapeshift between being an Eagle (strategist) and a Wolf (tactician) is crucial to realizing your desired future.

- Surround yourself with people who have the capacity to change rivers. Embrace the "no weak wolves" philosophy.

- The purpose of strategy is to provide you with a framework within which you can continually make choices that help you win.

- Continuous assessment of risk and reward can lead to great success.

- Strategy is an ongoing conversation that seeks confidence, not certainty.

TRY THIS:

Ask yourself who the Eagles and Wolves are in your life. Make a list of the Eagles who can help you get closer to your desired future. Then, make a list of the Wolves who can help you implement your desired future.

5

THE STRATEGY QUADRANT

"Building a visionary company requires 1 percent vision and 99 percent alignment."

JIM COLLINS & JERRY PORRAS

SOME YEARS AGO, we were preparing to welcome a group of entrepreneurs into one of our programs. The goal of the session that day was to develop an approach that helped attendees align their vision of what they wanted their life and business to look like in five to ten years with what they were currently doing daily, weekly, or monthly.

Feeling a bit stuck, my mentor and colleague Norm Trainor and I decided to take a break. We agreed that I would take what we were working on and play around for a bit. I wanted to develop something that served as a framework for thinking. Something that helped our clients have a better conversation about how they aligned strategy and tactics. What emerged was the Strategy Quadrant.

I had recently read *A Beautiful Constraint: How to Transform Your Limitations Into Advantages, and Why It's Everyone's Business* by Adam Morgan and Mark Barden. The basic premise of the book is that constraints give us freedom, and to demonstrate that idea, the authors referenced a wonderful study of how children use a playground. Researchers found that when you put a fence around a playground, children will use the entire space because they feel safe to play all the way to the edges. If, however, that fence is removed, creating a wide-open playground, the space the children choose to play in contracts. They stick to the middle of the playground and group together to feel safe.

In so many ways, success in life and business is about identifying your own beautiful constraints. When we developed the Strategy Quadrant, the goal was to design a framework our clients could use that gave them freedom while helping them play all the way to the edges. And from the first day we presented the Strategy Quadrant, it transformed how the professionals and entrepreneurs we worked with think about their life and their business.

I want you to think of the quadrant as the canvas on which you will sketch out your plan to achieve your desired future. Remember that, like strategy itself, models are imperfect and incomplete, and can always be improved. But they should at least be heuristically or prescriptively useful. By this I mean that models should help you problem-solve and/or offer you steps to follow. The Strategy Quadrant does both by helping you think within the context of what you want and providing you with steps you can follow to align and integrate your strategy with your tactics.

Many people's strategy plans fail because the dominant practice is to engage in a ritual or performance of strategic planning and then be done. Most people perform strategy but do not do strategy. History books are full of people, organizations, armies, and countries that failed or underperformed because they were unable to align their strategies and tactics. In some cases, their objectives were unclear. In others, they started with tactics and never used them to support a strategy.

The challenge with words like *strategy* and *tactics* is that people define them differently. If in the past you spent a lot of time on strategy plans only for them to sit on shelves, you will likely approach a strategy session with skepticism, and rightly so. Similarly, if you tend to be more tactical, you may tend to see the world only through a tactical lens. The Strategy Quadrant is a model for helping you to have better conversations about strategy and tactics—a playground that provides you with crucial boundaries so that you can play all the way to the edges.

The Future Drives the Present

In the business world, high performers tend to move readily from strategy to tactics, from planning to implementation. They are able to shift between the Eagle and Wolf mindsets so they can realize their desired future. If you want to build a successful business, a meaningful career, or a fulfilling life, the key is to align your long-term vision with the tasks that will be required daily, weekly, monthly, quarterly, and annually to achieve those goals. And that underscores the core concept of the Strategy Quadrant: that the future drives the present.

Behavioural psychology has taught us that we are all motivated to do things that have short-term, concrete benefits. We are motivated to do those things that are personal, immediate, and certain. We choose to eat the cookie instead of the apple. We go drinking with friends instead of going to the gym. These activities have results that are somewhat known and provide quick enjoyment or satisfaction.

The activities that are most likely to redefine our performance, however, are those that are future oriented and abstract; they are organizational, deferred, and even a gamble. For example, when you choose to go for a run instead of going for a meal with friends, you are likely to see the benefits in the future. Likewise, if you choose to eat at home more often, you may see larger savings that go toward your long-term goals.

We all fall victim to what behavioural psychologists refer to as present bias: when faced with trade-offs between immediate rewards and those that won't show up until the future, our tendency is to choose the immediate payoffs. The brain is wired to pay attention to things that are personal, immediate, and certain. As a result, we all need help in focusing on payoffs that are in the future.

Our research at The Covenant Group shows that the single most important determinant of your success and fulfillment in business and in life is the time frame in which you plan and work. High performers plan their work and work their plan differently than average producers, whether it's a long-range task or short-term, complex task. Where most people fall short is making sure that their short-term, complex tasks serve their desired futures. If you are brutally honest with yourself, what time horizon is informing your decisions?

Few of us can genuinely say our actions are informed by the things we want in ten years. So many of us find ourselves trapped by a present that is not serving the future we desire. The Strategy Quadrant can help you avoid three specific traps.

- **Trap 1:** Your strategy and tactics never meet.

- **Trap 2:** Your strategy and tactics sabotage each other.

- **Trap 3:** You start with tactics and never examine how what you do in the short term influences what you want, or even *if* you want a particular outcome in the long term.

So, with the idea in mind that your future drives your present, let me show you how the Strategy Quadrant is structured. But it's important to understand that while this appears to take a linear approach to strategy, it actually frames it as an iterative process.

Models should help you problem-solve and/or offer you steps to follow.

Drawing the Strategy Quadrant

The first step is to draw a timeline. The goal of this is to nudge you into thinking on a much longer time horizon. To get you to think about where you see yourself three to five years from now, maybe even ten to twenty years from now, and to work back from that point.

DRAWING THE STRATEGY QUADRANT, STEP 1

Remember that behavioural psychology has taught us that we are susceptible to present bias? This bias is completely tangible. I have seen it countless times with clients, and one example always sticks out for me. We were working with a client to develop his business plan. When we reached the point of implementing, he looked at me and said, "I know what I need to do, I just do not know if I want to pay for it. I always tell myself I will pay for it tomorrow and tomorrow never comes. So, I have been in the same spot for seven years."

In this case, the client's present bias was so strong that he had lost seven years to inaction. The short-term costs were keeping him from investing in the future he wanted and had mapped out. There is always a cost. There is a cost to doing nothing. There is a cost to taking action. Why not pay for the future you want?

The future drives the present, and it takes a leap of faith on your part to fully commit to an uncertain future. High performers raise the level of their gaze and place equal or greater emphasis on payoffs that are organizational, deferred, and a gamble. They are willing to forgo activities where the rewards are personal, immediate, and certain so they can focus on tasks that provide bigger future paybacks.

DRAWING THE STRATEGY QUADRANT, STEP 2

STRATEGY

	Q4	Q1	
SHORT TERM			**LONG TERM**
	Q3	Q2	

TACTICS

The horizontal line of the Strategy Quadrant is about getting you to think further out. Next, you need to integrate the strategy and tactics that will help you get what you want. This is the vertical axis of the Strategy Quadrant, the axis where you address things that are strategic and tactical. The top half of the quadrant focuses on the Eagle mindset (strategy). Here you are primarily concerned with what you want to achieve and why you want to achieve it. It is about zooming out and looking at your context from high above. Your Eagle mindset is about having a clear plan of action to achieve your goals.

The lower half of the quadrant refers to the Wolf mindset (tactics). The word *tactics* is derived from the ancient Greek word *taktikos*, which relates to the "art of arrangement," creating order, a system, or a mode of procedure. The Wolf mindset refers to how you implement or execute your strategy. Think of your tactics as the methods or procedures you use to achieve your objectives—your how-tos, activities, and tasks. The Wolf mindset is about zooming in and getting the job done.

Now that I've built the quadrant and created four zones, I label each zone like this:

Q1: Future Eagle
Q2: Today's Eagle
Q3: Today's Wolf
Q4: Future Wolf

And here's what the completed Strategy Quadrant looks like:

DRAWING THE STRATEGY QUADRANT, STEP 2

STRATEGY

TODAY'S EAGLE (Q2)	**FUTURE EAGLE** (Q1)
TODAY'S WOLF (Q3)	**FUTURE WOLF** (Q4)

SHORT TERM

LONG TERM

TACTICS

At a high level you want to think of each quadrant as follows:

Q1: Future Eagle is about your desired future. Where are you going and why are you going there? Where are you going to play to win?

Q2: Today's Eagle is about prioritization. What are the immediate choices you need to make to align you with your chosen direction?

Q3: Today's Wolf is about alignment. What are the immediate actions you need to take to help you get closer to your Future Eagle?

Q4: Future Wolf is about resource allocation. What structures, systems, and processes do you need to anticipate, plan, and prepare for when you realize your desired future?

The Strategy Quadrant in Practice

Let's use the streaming company Netflix as an example. Pretend for a moment that we were helping them build out their Strategy Quadrant. The first task is to define their Future Eagle. Roughly speaking, your Future Eagle is a combination of your long-term strategy and desired future. If you are a business owner, your desired future would be your business definition, which is made up of your vision, mission, values, operating principles, and business opportunity. Below is a hypothetical example of what a Strategy Quadrant designed for Netflix might look like.

TODAY'S EAGLE

- Prioritize member growth (more members = more data = more insights into what people will want to watch).
- Develop a strategic partnership framework for working with best-in-class content creators.

FUTURE EAGLE

Vision:

To be the #1 global streaming platform.

Strategy:
- Win Oscars with original content produced through strategic partnerships with creators.
- Use data to drive content creation and enable platform personalization.

TODAY'S WOLF

- Launch a new, high-quality original series or movie each month.
- Improve personalization and recommendations experience so users see more of what they want.
- Reduce churn by 5% and increase members by 8%.

FUTURE WOLF

- Enable content creators to autonomously produce diverse and inclusive content.
- Build a platform that leverages data so it creates an experience that is highly personalized and users love recommendations provided by the platform.

Now what would the Strategy Quadrant look like if you were using it to help you with your personal goals? Many of us have a goal to lose weight. My goal is to be able to play sports with my son fifteen years from now.

TODAY'S EAGLE	FUTURE EAGLE
• Focus on one area until it's mastered. For example, focus on getting the diet to a 9 out of 10 before focusing on something else. • Hire a trainer who has a community of people to help with accountability.	Vision: Lose weight to be healthy and able in the future. Strategy: • Focus on four core areas: sleep, diet, increasing muscle mass and flexibility, and improving cardiovascular capacity.
TODAY'S WOLF	**FUTURE WOLF**
• Clean out cupboards and start establishing specific routines for eating and exercising. • Measure daily health-related goals using tools like wearable technologies and scales that measure more than just weight.	• Focus on building systems to help stay on track. • Develop realistic quarterly and annual milestones to track progress. • Build a recipe book for all the most helpful meals. • Keep a record of the most enjoyable exercises.

Start and End with Your Future Eagle

The goal of the quadrant is to align the short-term tactical aspects of your desired future with the long-term strategic objectives. To do so, we need to examine each zone of the quadrant, starting with the longest task in which you are involved—your Future Eagle. If you are an entrepreneur, for example, your longest task is building a successful and sustainable business.

Most people make
plans and have
a performative
approach to strategy.

Using the Strategy Quadrant anchors you to your Future Eagle. This means that you should always be asking what I call your crucial alignment question:

Is this particular action (or tactic) in radical service of my Future Eagle?

If the answer is no, then you need to either delegate that task or stop doing it altogether. In applying the quadrant to your own business and life, the only rule you need to follow is to always start and end with the Future Eagle. In chapter 10, I will walk you through what this might look like. For now, keep in mind that you are turning strategy into an iterative process.

Keep Your Eye on the Fly

In today's technology-driven world, it is not a stretch to say that most of us are distracted by our devices, social media, emails, and text messages. One of the biggest benefits of the Strategy Quadrant is that it is a focusing tool. If you use the tool to get clear on what you need to do today to achieve your goals tomorrow, then it will help you clarify where and how you spend your time.

One of my favourite concepts from behavioural psychology is what anthropologist Mary Douglas called "matter out of place." The example most often used to explain this idea is the fly in the urinal. Architects were trying to find a way to improve hygiene in men's restrooms by reducing the number of times men missed the urinal. (I fully admit that it annoys me when men miss a urinal. How distracted do you have to be to miss a sink that you are standing in front of? But I digress.)

In their quest to reduce the spillage, the architects placed an image of a fly in the urinal. Another variation of this is using a small goalpost with a hanging ball or painting a target in the urinal. No matter the technique, when men came across these designs, it kicked them out of autopilot and spurred them to aim at the fly, the target, or the goalpost. This simple yet elegant solution reduced the amount of urine on the restroom floors by 80 percent! It also reduced the cost of cleaning by 8 percent.

We all go on autopilot from time to time, so having a technique that jolts us out of our automation is helpful. Many of our clients have described the alignment question—does this serve my Future Eagle?—as a profound way to jolt themselves out of distraction and point them toward more intentional actions. The Strategy Quadrant is both a tool that can be applied and one that can help you think about your next course of action. If you are about to take an action and it does not align with your Future Eagle, you simply don't go there.

Many people come to us because they are trapped in a life that is dictated by urgent tasks that seem to be constant. Thinking about the beautiful constraints in the playground that started this chapter, you can see the Strategy Quadrant as a way to help you frame the boundaries within which you will play. As much as possible, you want to use the full playground so that you can identify your purpose and then design systems, processes, and approaches that will bring into alignment everything you do. That's how to reach your goals.

REFLECTION POINTS

- Every action has a cost. Invest in the future you want.

- Make sure what you are doing in the short term is serving your desired future.

- Start and end with your Future Eagle and anchor all your actions to it.

- Turn your strategy into an iterative planning process.

TRY THIS:

1   Take some time now to write a paragraph or two that describes your desired future. In the next chapter you will build on this exercise.

2   How might you use the "matter out of place" tool in your own life? For example, I always used to forget to turn off my computer monitors, but I never forgot to turn off the lights. My solution was to put a sticker of a wolf next to the light switch. Now every time I turn off the lights, I see the sticker of the wolf and I remember to turn off my monitors.

For helpful tools and resources, visit keitademming.com or scan the QR code below.

6

FUTURE EAGLE

"If one does not know to which port
one is sailing, no wind is favourable."

SENECA

STRATEGY QUADRANT, FUTURE EAGLE

STRATEGY

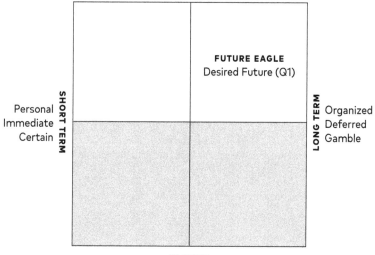

FUTURE EAGLE
Desired Future (Q1)

Personal
Immediate
Certain

SHORT TERM

LONG TERM

Organized
Deferred
Gamble

TACTICS

FUTURE EAGLE is about what you want and where you want to go—your desired future. If you are a business leader or entrepreneur looking at improving your business growth, the Future Eagle quadrant is where you define and clarify the business vision, mission, values, operating principles, and opportunities. All of that should go into your strategy creation.

Defining your Future Eagle is an iterative process, so be prepared to revisit this quadrant constantly because it is your anchor. Think about your Future Eagle as a combination of your strategy to win combined with the future you want. Below are some examples of how that would look.

Here is the Future Eagle of an individual who wants to become a financial advisor.

Desired Future: Jolie unexpectedly lost her husband, Paul, in a boating accident. While he was alive, they had many arguments over the life insurance premiums they were paying. Until the accident, Jolie had deemed it an unnecessary expense. After the death of her husband, she realized how wrong she was. Had it not been for the insurance Paul had insisted on, Jolie and her children would not have been able to afford their lifestyle. Today, Jolie is on a mission to ensure every couple she knows is prepared for whatever life may throw at them.

Strategy: Jolie plans to direct her financial advice primarily to women. Her strategy is to hold women-focused educational events. At each event she plans to share her story to show women how important financial planning is.

According to *Forbes*, Rihanna grew her brand Fenty Beauty into a $2.8 billion company. Here is what her Future Eagle might have looked like.

Desired Future: Build an inclusive global brand that serves and celebrates people of all shapes and sizes. Rihanna launched the brand "so that people everywhere would be included." She was inspired to create the brand because she saw a void in the industry for products that worked for all skin types and tones.

Strategy: Focus on areas that her competitors did not or were not willing to. Leverage her celebrity status and audience to build brand awareness. Focus the advertising on regular people and not on traditional model-like bodies.

And here is the possible Future Eagle of B Lab, the organization behind the Benefit Corporation certificate.

Desired Future: In 2006, a group of entrepreneurs had a vision to create an organization that would certify companies who were interested in being the best not only in the world, but also *for* the world. B Lab certifies companies as B Corporations as a way of creating organizations that are committed to high standards of accountability, transparency, and social and environmental performance.

Strategy: To use a rigorous certification process to build a community of values-driven companies.

The key concepts covered in this chapter are designed to help you orient your thinking around the future you desire and the strategy you plan to use as you navigate this quadrant.

Who Do You Serve?

Start from the outside in. What that means is that you should always focus on the people you serve and do what is in the best interest of your client. Let me give you an example of how not doing so can adversely affect your business strategy.

The "League Table" was a ranking system of success rates for in vitro fertilization (IVF) clinics throughout the United Kingdom. The objective was to provide consumers with a way to make informed decisions about which clinics they should choose. Clinic success rates were driven by two main factors: the skill of the practitioners and the age, health, and fertility of the clinic's patients. Success was easy to measure: Did the procedure result in birth or not?

Unfortunately, one group of clinics chose to game the system in pursuit of quick success. They adopted a practice referred to as selection at the gate. They selected women who were young, had not unsuccessfully tried IVF in the past, and had lots of eggs to "harvest" (not my language). The clinics that chose easy cases saw a small increase in success rates in the short term.

A second group of clinics accepted whoever showed up at their doors, and initially these clinics performed worse than those clinics who selected easy clients at the gate. Over the long term, however, the second group of clinics began to outperform the first group. They were taking on difficult cases and learning from them. Over time they outperformed the clinics that took on only easy cases. Lesson learned? When you are thinking about your business strategy, you first need to serve and understand your clients.

Raise the Level of Your Gaze

So few people are willing to play the long game that simply changing the level of your gaze sets you apart from the crowd.

When Amazon founder Jeff Bezos spoke with *Wired* magazine in 2011, he said, "If everything you do needs to work on a three-year time horizon, then you're competing against a lot of people. If you're willing to invest on a seven-year time horizon, you're now competing against a fraction of those people, because very few companies are willing to do that. Just by lengthening the time horizon, you can engage in endeavours that you could never otherwise pursue." Playing a long game, though, means that you will likely need to give up some short-term gains. Take our client Jason Boudreau, for example.

Jason was a thirty-year-old financial advisor with a part-time assistant when we started working with him. His company, VELA Wealth, was already successful, but Jason wanted to realize his potential. One of Jason's mentors while he was growing up and during his early adulthood was John Nicola, the founder and CEO of Nicola Wealth, one of the pre-eminent wealth management firms in Canada. Jason greatly respected John's achievements. John Nicola communicates in the language of the Future Eagle because he focuses on vision and strategy. And when he speaks, people listen. He is exceptionally gifted at outlining a clear plan of action to achieve what is important in the next one, five, ten years.

The two most important indicators of what we value are how we spend our time and how we spend our money. Early in our work together, we asked Jason three questions:

- What will you be doing ten years from now?
- How much income will you be generating?
- How would you describe the quality of your life?

Jason had a clear vision of where he wanted to go: he wanted to build something similar to Nicola Wealth. He also told us that in ten years he would be earning a seven-figure income as the CEO of a multimillion-dollar financial advisory firm with a strong team of committed individuals who are passionate about making a difference in the lives of their clients.

Like many high performers, Jason also realized that it is not what you want in life that is important, it is what you are willing to give up. At one point Jason decided to change the structure of his organization and how he was compensated. This meant two things. First, while he was changing the structure of the company it would bring in less revenue, but in three years the company would significantly grow its revenue. Second, by changing the compensation structure in his company, Jason had to take a pay cut in the short term. Jason took these steps so that he could structure the organization for growth. He was willing to pay the short-term cost for the long-term gain.

Jason was clear about his Future Eagle. He played a long game and was crystal clear about the time frame around what he wanted to do. He invested time and money in the areas of his life and work that were important to him and the people he cares about. He had a strong sense of purpose and was building a business that would make a difference and be a sustainable enterprise over time.

No surprise then that today Jason is earning a seven-figure income and running a multimillion-dollar financial advisory firm with a strong committed team. And he achieved all of this in six years.

When I give talks, I often emphasize that before we can go anywhere, we need an address. If a friend is going to give you a ride somewhere, they are going to need the address. Your Future Eagle is your desired destination. It is a clear picture of where you want to be five to ten years from now. Once you

It is not what you want in life that is important, it is what you are willing to give up.

are clear on where you are going and how you are going to win, you can then decide how you are going to get there. And, as Jeff Bezos points out, the further out you extend your time frame, the fewer people you will be competing against.

Inform Your Strategy with Your Vision and Mission

Getting clear on your Future Eagle is a process that asks some key questions and then asks you to consider how your strategy reflects the answers. Granted, these are big questions, and it's not within the scope of this book to answer them for you. That should be done in conversation with yourself and your team. But that is what the Future Eagle quadrant is all about: asking questions so that you can better design your business strategy. Here is the thinking process that leads to your Future Eagle:

1 What is your vision? Vision answers the question, Where are you going? It is a mental picture of your desired future.

2 What is your mission? Mission answers the questions, What is your purpose? What problem do you wish to solve? What standard will you hold yourself to?

3 Your strategy should evolve out of your vision and mission.

In today's world, a mission or purpose is a strategic differentiator for many companies. One of the most inspiring examples of a company that is absolutely committed to their mission and vision is the outdoor clothing retailer Patagonia. Patagonia's mission statement used to read, "Build the best product, cause no unnecessary harm, utilize business to inspire and implement solutions to the environmental issue." They have since updated it to read, "We're in business to save our home planet." This mission statement is driven by four core values:

1 Build the best product.
2 Cause no unnecessary harm.
3 Use business to protect nature.
4 Not bound by convention.

The company is so dedicated to its mission and values that in 2022 its founder, Yvon Chouinard, announced, "Earth is now our only shareholder." The company is now so committed to its Future Eagle that it has developed a unique approach to business. In a letter on the Patagonia website, Chouinard wrote, "Truth be told, there were no good options available. So, we created our own." As Chouinard explained, "100% of the company's voting stock transfers to the Patagonia Purpose Trust, created to protect the company's values; and 100% of the nonvoting stock has been given to the Holdfast Collective, a non-profit dedicated to fighting the environmental crisis and defending nature. The funding will come from Patagonia: Each year, the money we make after reinvesting in the business will be distributed as a dividend to help fight the crisis."

Once you have defined your mission and vision, your strategy should be your best hypothesis of how you are going to accomplish your mission and vision so you can create value for the people you choose to serve. Think of it as your simple guideline that informs everything you do.

Using Simple Guidelines to Develop Strategy

I have several guidelines I use to stay on top of things. One rule is that I should touch things once. So, if I pick up mail, I want to read it, file it, or recycle it the first time I touch it.

There is tremendous value in evoking simple guidelines as you develop your strategy and find ways to create value for the people you wish to serve. When we address complex problems, there is a natural tendency for us to seek complex solutions, but simple guidelines provide better results. Simple guidelines can be powerful business tools.

Ian Telfer is a friend of The Covenant Group and one of Canada's top business minds. He has a wonderful and simple guideline: red flags never go down. He uses this as a reminder to look for red flags and then to act on them. My friend and mentor Richard Bell is a serial entrepreneur who has founded several successful companies. Bell has a simple guideline when it comes to customer service. He tells his team that when they are dealing with disgruntled clients, they should do what they would do if the person were their grandmother. It's a genius customer service rule.

A classic example of simple guidelines can be found in hospitals around the world. Instead of treating patients on a first come, first served basis, hospitals use the triage method, a practice that originated during the Napoleonic wars and was refined during World War II. The general idea is that patients are assigned colour codes:

- Green for the walking wounded: people whose treatment can be safely delayed.

- Yellow for injuries that are more urgent but not a top priority.

- Red for people who have injuries that cannot wait.

- Black for people who are unlikely to survive even with the best of efforts. These folks are sent for palliative care.

Your mission and vision should serve as a simple guideline that informs everything you do. Additionally, you should look for places in your life and work to develop and apply simple guidelines. For example, I am from Trinidad and Tobago and we Caribbean people have a reputation for being late. A family friend taught me a simple life rule: never be late for something that can leave you. He was referring to things like a flight, a cruise ship, or a bus. It is a simple rule that he applies in his life, and it works for him within his cultural context. I cannot say if he is late for everything else, but I do know he is not late for things that can leave him.

Create Value for Those You Serve

Earlier I talked about how important it is to understand and serve your client. In terms of strategy, the key way to think about this is to ask, How will I create value for the people I wish to serve? If you can answer this question, and you are confident that it puts you in a position to win, you have strengthened your strategy.

In their book *Simple Rules: How to Thrive in a Complex World*, Harvard professors Donald Sull and Kathleen Eisenhardt tell the story of how CEO Alex Behring developed a simple-guideline strategy to win. Behring was hired by a private equity firm to turn around America Latina Logistica (ALL). The task was to turn around a portion of a government-run railroad network the firm had recently bought. Years of chronic underfunding meant the railroad network was in poor shape. Most of its revenue was generated during a few months of the year when soybean farmers shipped their harvest to the market. But the company was often forced to turn farmers away because many of the tracks were damaged or they did not have the capacity to ship the goods. It was a losing scenario for everyone. Farmers watched their crops rot in the fields while ALL turned away business.

Behring needed to find a way to prioritize how the company would allocate its resources. He and his team needed to focus on two things: creating alignment across the organization and generating revenue. Behring needed a strategy that was easy to implement and would provide his team with the constraints within which they could play.

Talk about being in a difficult spot. Behring had only $15 million for capital spending, while his managers had requested ten times that. The company had received little investment in years, so almost all proposed projects had merit. Behring decided to bring together a diverse team of managers from across the company. Their task was to come up with simple guidelines that would help them select the proposals to be funded. The team came up with a set of guidelines to help them do so:

1 Remove bottlenecks to grow revenue.
2 Provide immediate benefits.
3 Minimize up-front expenditure.
4 Wherever possible, reuse existing resources.

The rules were clear, straightforward, and simple. They were shared across the company and employees at any level could develop ideas that fit the strategy. Most of their competitors outspent them, but ALL won using strategy. For example, one frontline employee proposed the idea of increasing the size of fuel tanks as a way of extending the distance trains could travel before needing to refuel. This reduced downtime and increased revenue immediately.

The brilliance of this approach was that Behring had found a way to operationalize his strategy. Strategy can be defined as the alignment of outputs and objectives, capabilities and resources, with the opportunities and challenges the environment provides. When Behring developed his simple guidelines to inform which projects would be funded, he was implementing a strategy in this way.

Within three years, ALL increased revenue by 50 percent and tripled operating cash flow while maintaining the best safety record of all the freight lines in the country. What is great about Behring's approach is that he found a way to engage the employees. Using simple guidelines, he turned the company around and beat their competitors using frontline innovation. In using constraints, he found a way to help his team play all the way to the edges.

In some literature about creating strategy, the focus is on beating your competition. But focusing on beating your competition will produce a strategy that is different from focusing on winning. You can beat who you think is your competition and still lose. If, however, you focus on winning with the people you serve, you win. Tempting as it may be to focus on beating the competition, the moment you do so, you are no longer serving your clients. It can also be tempting to copy your competition, but doing so also means you are no longer being strategic.

When you find a way to win, particularly when you want to create value for your stakeholders, your competition becomes irrelevant. This is not to say there is no value in looking at what your competition is doing. However, your strategic advantage will likely come from focusing on the people you wish to serve. The emphasis should be on playing a game that puts you in a position to win. But once you've built your strategic hypothesis that sets you up for the win, remember to not get locked in, because the world is not static.

Treat Your Strategy as a Hypothesis

As you navigate your Future Eagle quadrant, you will need to remind yourself constantly that all businesses are built on a set of assumptions. The longer the business is in the market, the more these assumptions are tested. But many entrepreneurs struggle when the underlying assumption of their business and their strategy changes—they want to stay the course. However, if your assumptions change, you should consider changing your strategy to reflect those changes because strategy is a hypothesis that you test. You test your strategy in the Today's Wolf mindset, and we will explore this more in chapter 8. For now, hold that thought while we explore this idea of strategy as a hypothesis or temporary holding position.

Today, Play-Doh is a billion-dollar children's product, but originally it was designed and sold to help remove coal residue. When, for various reasons, the demand for the product dropped, the company learned of a schoolteacher in Cincinnati who was using it in her arts and crafts class as a form of clay. The company quickly produced some colourful versions of the product and sold it as a kid's toy. Now it's a staple in childhood arts and craft activities. The people behind Play-Doh were willing to test a new hypothesis and experiment in the market.

As I said earlier, it's important to keep coming back to your Future Eagle quadrant to examine it when things don't work out as you thought they might. Testing your strategy can result in some unique gains. Malika, a nurse-turned-financial advisor, was successful in winning clients such as nurses and other professionals to her business. But her goal was to land fifteen to twenty doctors as clients over a two-year period. Malika decided to undertake a campaign targeted at doctors. She used direct mail, contacted their receptionists, met with doctors she had worked with in the past, and even organized workshops targeted at doctors. She got a few meetings, but not one doctor became a client. After six months of work, she still did not have any doctors as clients.

Part of the challenge was that Malika had chosen to market to a small target group—a group of people who, it is often said, think of themselves as second only to God. As a former nurse, Malika was working against a strong cultural dynamic, so if she wanted to go after doctors, she needed an indirect approach.

Malika developed a marketing campaign directed at the people who were comfortable speaking with her, such as nursing supervisors, hospital administrative staff, medical technicians, and, of course, the nurses. She leveraged her contacts for personal introductions, offered "lunch and learn" seminars to hospital staff (including a couple at midnight right after shift change), and arranged to write a regular column on financial fitness in the hospital's internal newsletter. She volunteered everywhere in the medical community—at charity events, on a committee to attract new doctors, and in fundraising activities.

Using these approaches, Malika was able to gain a number of new clients. Since many of these clients worked alongside the doctors, it wasn't long before word of mouth provided her with the access and respect that had eluded her. Six months later, Malika was an acknowledged financial expert in the health care industry. Not surprisingly, several doctors noticed what she was doing. Over the next eighteen months, Malika was able to onboard twelve doctors as clients.

When you develop your strategy, you do so based on a set of assumptions. Malika assumed that she could target doctors directly. She had a hypothesis and when she tested it, she learned that she was wrong. So, she changed course and recalibrated her strategy to set herself up for a win. (Note that Malika was testing her hypothesis in Wolf mode, not in Eagle mode. Using the Strategy Quadrant is an iterative process.)

Turn Your Strategy Statement Into Questions

You've probably noticed that navigating the quadrant of the Future Eagle means asking and answering a lot of questions.

The first time I noticed that the word "questions" had the word "quest" in it, it entirely changed how I view questions. Questions take us on a journey or quest, and like philosopher Bertrand Russell once said, "In all affairs it's a healthy thing now and then to hang a question mark on things you take for granted." Most companies work toward creating a strategy statement. I want to encourage you to start with a strategy question. Why? Because when creating strategy there are many things we take for granted or assume. Questions encourage us to test our assumptions. Framing your strategy statement as a question encourages you to go look for better approaches.

Roger Martin, one of the world's foremost thinkers on strategy, popularized the "what must be true" question. For example, suppose you want to grow your business by 20 percent; you then ask, What must be true for me to achieve that? I have always found asking what must be true to be an important question in developing strategy. More importantly, the question serves as a guide in helping us make choices and notice what is or is not working.

Here is where I get philosophical. Earlier I told you that the antidote to complexity is inquiry (chapter 3). In a complex world it is much more helpful to frame your statements as questions. A statement signals the end of thinking, the end of questioning, the end of a conversation. To keep the conversation going, you need to ask more and better questions.

Martin also proposes that there are three strategy questions you need to answer clearly:

1 Where are you going to play to win?
2 Why are you going to play there?
3 How are you going to win?

Notice that these questions nudge you toward learning and exploration. The Future Eagle quadrant helps you enter an ongoing conversation that answers your key strategic questions.

For one team I worked with, moving from a statement to a question turned things around. They were relentlessly focused on engaging their userbase for eighteen months, to moderate success. When I asked them to frame their statement as a question, it got them to think of new ways to engage their userbase. Instead of operating from the mindset of "we will turn around the company by engaging our userbase," they asked, "Are we winning by engaging our userbase? How do we know we are winning? How else might we engage our userbase?"

Reframing their statements as questions nudged them to think of five new ways to engage their userbase and generated more creative ideas. The first few ideas got them such strong results that they doubled down on using questions as their default approach to improving and iterating on their strategy and ultimately the product.

Similarly, remember my brother the mechanic? He worked for a luxury dealer in Trinidad and Tobago and once told me a story of a car that had bounced between the mechanical department and the electrical department (don't ask me the difference between those two). In each department, they ran diagnostic tools on the car and in each case the diagnostic report suggested that a new part or repair was needed. In the end, the dealership ended up ordering several new parts and they tried several things to repair the problem. But nothing worked.

When the car got to my brother, he started by asking basic questions before reaching for the diagnostic tools. He checked the fuses, changed them, and fixed the problem in a few minutes, much to the annoyance of his colleagues in the other departments. My brother is the kind of mechanic who can listen to a car engine and tell you what is wrong with it. He frequently goes on rants about mechanics who cannot do their jobs because they depend on diagnostic tools. He cautions that although these tools are helpful and can save time, a mechanic's best tool is to ask the right questions before reaching for the so-called right tool.

A strategy statement does not help you seek better answers and approaches—it locks you into that statement. Questions help us treat our strategy as a hypothesis, a temporary holding position. If your assumptions change, you change your strategy. Questions help you clarify your Future Eagle, so here are some expansive questions to help get you thinking about your Future Eagle business strategy:

- How are you going to create value for your ideal client?
- Why might your client choose you over the competition?
- What must be true?
- What will you notice when you start winning?
- Are you doing what you set out to do?

IN A complex world, things are ever-changing. Even though you may have arrived at some strategic hypothesis in the Future Eagle quadrant, you cannot know if your strategy will work until you put it into practice. The Strategy Quadrant provides a framework for you to design and implement your desired future. The challenge is learning how to bring your strategy into the present.

In the next chapter, I will talk about Today's Eagle. This quadrant is where you focus on those things that are short-term and strategic to make sure that the activities and tasks you undertake daily are aligned with your desired future.

REFLECTION POINTS

- Serve your client first and make sure your strategy creates value for them.

- Raise the level of your gaze by looking at a longer time horizon.

- Use your company's vision and mission to inform your strategy hypothesis and as a simple guideline for everything you do.

- Turn your strategy statements into questions in a quest to find better answers and approaches.

- Test your strategic hypothesis and be ready to change course if needed.

TRY THIS:

Defining your Future Eagle begins with clarity about where you want to go. Answer these questions as you sketch out your own Future Eagle.

1 What will you be doing ten years from now?

2 How much income will you be earning?

3 How would you describe the quality of your life ten years from now?

7

TODAY'S EAGLE

"The essence of strategy is
choosing what not to do."

MICHAEL E. PORTER

STRATEGY QUADRANT, TODAY'S EAGLE

STRATEGY

TODAY'S EAGLE
Prioritization (Q2)

Personal
Immediate
Certain

SHORT TERM

LONG TERM

Organized
Deferred
Gamble

TACTICS

T HE FUTURE Eagle quadrant works with abstract concepts, the long-term choices that define your performance and are organizational, deferred, and a gamble. Once you move from Future Eagle to the Today's Eagle quadrant, you move toward thinking about short-term choices that are personal, immediate, and certain. Here you will need to prioritize the choices that will get you to your desired future.

There are few places on earth that expose the tension between short-term and long-term choices like a university campus. When I was in university, I found myself on academic probation. My past defined me as a dyslexic athlete who had not graduated from high school. If I had any hopes of attending university, I needed to complete a university transfer program. I decided to attend Capilano College (now Capilano University) near Vancouver. I worked hard, got excellent grades, and was accepted into the University of British Columbia. But once I got to UBC, I was lost, unfocused, and distracted because I had no goals, and I wasn't making my studies a priority.

In North America, a university degree can take four to five years to complete. But beside your coursework, university life comes with countless fun distractions. There are parties to go to, people to meet, clubs to join, sports to play, romances to pursue, and bars to drink at. Taking advantage of all this university life is how I found myself in a situation that threatened my chances to graduate. And if I got kicked out, I would need to explain that to my Caribbean parents. I was on a burning bridge.

A few things contributed to my failing grades. Initially, I had set a finite goal: to get grades good enough to move from a community college to university. But once I got there, I was floundering. I was also in a stormy relationship, and I often spent days cleaning up my emotions. Rarely was I productive on those days. This experience taught me that a stable personal life is directly related to a stable and successful professional life. Things were not good, and I was wasting time that I should have been using to focus on my desired future.

I eventually decided to exit that relationship and landed on the goal of working toward becoming an adult educator who transformed the lives of the people he served. This was me getting clear on my Future Eagle, my mission and vision. I had a port to sail toward. I knew why I was getting up each day. To complete my Future Eagle, I needed to develop a strategy. My goal was to learn as much as I could about human performance and learning. It became my purpose and obsession. The goal I set in university is still my goal today.

Things turned around for me when I was able to develop and implement short-term strategies that helped me achieve my desired future. This was me clarifying my Today's Eagle. I put rules around relationships so they did not distract my focus on school. I scheduled my week so that my studying time was a number one priority. At the start of the semester, I filled up my calendar with two-hour study time slots for every hour of class and treated each of them like a meeting with a billionaire. I showed up to every class on time and never left early. That semester I got the first four A's I ever had in my life. For my parents, the fact I was attending university was already a small miracle. In their eyes, these marks were yet another miracle; they had simply hoped that I would one day graduate.

What I did not understand at the time is that I had set a finite goal. Finite goals are like the ones athletes often make, such as deciding they want to win the Olympic 100 metres.

That is different from deciding they want to be the best sprinter the world has ever seen. An infinite goal strives toward mastery, while a finite goal has a clear ending and is something specific to be accomplished. In my case, I used four key strategies to guide everything I did to get off academic probation:

1 I developed an infinite goal.
2 I aligned my finite goals with my infinite goal.
3 I ensured my personal life supported my professional/academic life.
4 I designed my day.

TODAY'S EAGLE

- Align my finite goals with my infinite goals.
- Ensure my personal life supports my professional/academic life.
- Design my day.

FUTURE EAGLE

Vision:

Become an expert on human performance and learning.

Strategy:
- Learn as much as I can about human performance. Focus on the areas where I see the most potential.
- Determine my infinite goals.

TODAY'S WOLF

- Build my calendar at the start of each semester including all my classes and the two hours of study for each hour of class.
- Develop a practice of reviewing my calendar at the start of the week and first thing in the morning.
- Ensure my calendar is on my phone and follow it.
- Find myself a study group with similar goals.

FUTURE WOLF

- Develop a rough calendar that maps out my entire year and provides me with a good sense of schedule for the rest of my degree.
- Gather a group of friends who act as my accountability group.

The table on the previous page is what my Strategy Quadrant might have looked like at the time. There are two things to note: Back then, using a calendar on your phone was not as easy as it is today. And it is important to know that the timelines for the Future Eagle and Future Wolf are different from those in the business world, given that most universities operate on a four-month timeline.

Infinite goals inform our short-term strategies, but finite goals are needed as well. The goals you set in your Future Eagle should be infinite goals. The goals you set in your Today's Eagle are often finite. But the most important distinction is that your finite goals should be in service of your infinite goals. The mistake we see often is that people are unclear about how to focus their time and energy. I have learned it is important to start by helping clients realize where their focus adds the most value.

At The Covenant Group, we use an exercise called the three R's (I will explain this exercise in depth later in this chapter) to help clients realize where they add the most value. As a precursor to that exercise, I often ask these three questions because I have found it helpful for clients get clear on these things early on:

1 What is the best use of your time?
2 What value do you bring to your organization?
3 Who do you wish to serve?

How Do You Use Your Time?

Nassor, one of our clients, ran a reasonably successful business but struggled in the role of CEO. He did not like it, nor did he think he was particularly good at it. He was, however, the major shareholder in the business, so it made sense for him to be the CEO.

When Nassor thought about the role he wanted to play, he realized he could add the most value as head of marketing. He decided to find someone who could run the company, and he would focus on marketing. When he found the right person to replace him as CEO, he made the move. Together Nassor and his new CEO were able to grow the company by 40 percent because Nassor was working at his highest potential, and so too was his CEO. A few years later, Nassor sold his company to a larger organization.

If you return to the original alignment question in chapter 5—is the action or decision I am about to make in service of my Future Eagle?—that will help you zero in on those things that are strategic and short term. And as you think about your short-term strategies, bear in mind these two principles: optimization and leverage.

- Optimization refers to the best and most effective use of your talents, your natural abilities. You focus on working at the highest level of your capabilities. This means you do only what only you can do and do it well. You delegate the rest. This is where being able to say no is really important. Saying no defines who you are!

- Leverage refers to focusing on what you do best and leveraging the rest. People who leverage well use as many of the capabilities and resources available to them as they can. They use the time, energy, creativity, and intelligence of others so they are free to apply their unique talents to the tasks where they excel.

Let me use Nassor's example to break down Today's Eagle thinking. Nassor knew that he was struggling in the role of CEO and that this was compromising the future of his company overall. So, he asked himself this question: In the next three to fifteen months, what must be true for me to achieve my Future Eagle of growing the business? He realized that if he was going to make his business grow, he needed to change what he was doing. He needed to work at the highest level of his capability, but as the company owner, he wondered what people would think if he hired someone else to be the CEO and appeared to demote himself to head of marketing. But in the end, Nassor knew that if his goal was to the grow the company, he needed to get clear on what he would start doing, stop doing, and continue doing, and why these approaches would help him achieve his goals.

- Is my CEO role the best use of my time?

- What is the best next step toward working at the highest level of my capability?

- What should I say no to?

Figuring out your short-term strategies, your Today's Eagle, hinges on asking yourself, Where do I add or create the most value? This is not about what you like to do. In Nassor's case, he asked himself the three questions.

Now it's your turn: Take the time to think about where you contribute the most value in your daily tasks. Find five people in your circle who you trust to give you honest feedback. Ask for their input on where they think you contribute and create the most value.

Identifying the Three R's

A number of years ago, we worked with Omari, a lawyer who is a good example of the power of aligning your Future Eagle with Today's Eagle. When we began coaching Omari, he was burned out from working many hours on unprofitable cases and running from court to court. He had no strategy and reacted to whatever cases came his way. Initially, Omari thought he needed to change professions so he could make more money. But what he realized was that he instead needed to learn how to build a successful law practice.

Here is how we helped Omari achieve that goal. The quadrant of Today's Eagle asks you to clarify issues around how your business operates so that you can plan how to build it successfully. Part of that clarification process involves identifying the three R's that I will outline next. Our experience at The Covenant Group has shown us that most people get one or more of these priorities wrong.

1 Who is the Right Client?
2 What is the Right Value Proposition?
3 What is the Right Exchange of Value (Right Price)?

We suggested to Omari that if he could answer these three questions, he would have greater success and fulfillment without having to change his career.

Who Is The Right Client?

Many clients we meet struggle to clearly articulate their Right Client because most of them simply have not spent time thinking about who they wish to serve. Your Right Client is a hypothetical example of the perfect client, which includes both their demographic characteristics—age, income, net worth, marital status, type of employment, and location—as well as their psychographic characteristics, such as attitudes and aspirations. At The Covenant Group, we recommend that you identify five demographic factors and five psychographic factors to paint as complete a picture of your ideal client profile as possible. In my experience, it is incredibly important to ensure that the psychographic factors of the client are aligned with your own values.

Here's how that might look: Bello was a young plumber who wanted to grow his business. He knew he wanted to work with young families who lived in his neighbourhood. He wanted to work with people he liked and families who he could grow with over time. He wanted them to live close enough to his house so that if they had emergencies, he could easily service them. Bello defined his Right Client as:

DEMOGRAPHIC	PSYCHOGRAPHIC
• Young family with children	• Loyal
• Household income greater than $150,000	• Friendly
• Value quality over price
• Lives within 20 minutes of his house	• Ambitious
• Generous of spirit
• Homeowners	
• Age: 30–50	

Returning to Omari: he needed to think about who his Right Client was. At the time, that was anyone who walked through his door. He took on many legal aid cases and this lack of selectivity was causing Omari to burn out. He was always busy, working many hours, with little time for family and friends. Omari's business model was not working for him. But once he came to understand that his Right Client was someone who could pay a retainer of at least $20,000, he was in a position to address his Right Value Proposition.

You need
to reorganize,
restructure,
or redefine your
business.

What is the Right Value Proposition?

To attract the right clients, high performers put a lot of thought into the Right Value Proposition because the clarity of your value proposition drives everything. Your starting point is to understand how you communicate your value to your clients. Why should someone take time out of their day to meet with you or engage with your product? Most people demonstrate their value proposition in how they answer the question, What do you do?

Omari, like many of the people we work with, had not described what made him unique in the legal world. He had not articulated his value proposition in a simple and compelling manner. One of Omari's distinguishing characteristics is his ability to deal with complex cases. He devotes the time, energy, creativity, and intelligence to effectively address these cases. As a result, his success rate in court is extremely high—and that is part of his value proposition. Identifying his value proposition has led to building his brand in such a way that he attracts clients who fit his Right Client profile. He recognized that he was at his best when he was working on a few high-value cases. In other words, he would work with a limited number of clients who could pay a $20,000 retainer to get the best legal mind working for them.

For Marcus Mackay, a client who started out as a personal trainer and founded a company called M Perform, his value proposition is that he takes you from survival mode to thrive mode so that you can live life in a body you love. My value proposition is I help individuals and teams be better business-people and better people in business. For the Right Client, your value proposition resonates deeply and causes the listener to say, "That's interesting. Tell me more!"

Your value proposition should be informed by three questions:

1 What makes you relevant?
2 What makes you different?
3 What makes you sustainable?

Marcus built a company that helps his clients work out at home. His insight was that there are 168 hours in a week and as a personal trainer he would see his clients for only three to four hours a week. That meant his clients had 164 hours to undo all the work they had done together. So Marcus created an online training company that focuses on supporting his clients 168 hours a week. He focused on coaching the whole person so they could thrive in a body they loved. This made him relevant, different, and sustainable. Everything he and his team do is driven by their value proposition.

High performers help their prospects and clients identify, clarify, and intensify what is important to them. They demonstrate their value to their client quickly. They put a lot of effort into uncovering what the people they serve want. They use stories, analogies, and metaphors to highlight the risks to which their profile clients are exposed and the ways in which their services eliminate or mitigate losses. They establish confidence by showing profile prospects and clients the relevance and uniqueness of their value proposition.

What is the Right Exchange of Value?

People want to feel that they are getting a fair exchange of value. Entrepreneurs need to price their products and services appropriately to ensure the financial viability of the business. People will pay more for a product or service if it provides benefits that they value. So, the Right Exchange of Value addresses the benefits to the client of working with you and what you derive in return.

Omari had many legal aid cases, but they paid on the low end of the fee spectrum. To get the Right Exchange of Value, Omari needed to stop doing so much low-value legal work—he had to say no so he could focus on what he was best at. We wanted to work on limiting his client load to those who could pay a $20,000 retainer for his high-quality legal services. This would allow him to take on fewer clients, leaving more time in his life. He had to focus on quality of activity, rather than simply quantity. Today, Omari has a very manageable practice. He is able to work with clients who can pay his preferred retainer and devote himself entirely to a few cases. This was the Right Exchange of Value for him and his clients.

Omari wanted more than just money in his career. He wanted to live life fully and he has achieved this by redesigning his practice to facilitate what is important in his life. He also learned that every business reaches a ceiling. Once you hit that ceiling, what you did to get you to that point no longer works to take you to the next level. You need to reorganize, restructure, or redefine your business. Omari is now working at his highest potential, serving his Right Client, and receiving the Right Exchange of Value for his service.

AFTER OMARI went through the process of answering his three R's, he returned to the practice of law rather than change career, as he initially thought he would have to. Over the next two years he tripled his income. Omari wanted to build a business that not only was about making money, but also fulfilled his values. Omari's short-term strategy (Today's Eagle) was turning down business even if he needed the money. His Today's Eagle was about saying yes to those clients that fit his ideal client profile.

Your task is to find the short-term strategies that help align your desired future with your actions. Start by articulating your Future Eagle. Then prioritize the short-term strategies, your Today's Eagle, that will help you get there.

In the next chapter I explore Today's Wolf, those things that are tactical and short term.

REFLECTION POINTS

- Prioritization is the name of the game in Today's Eagle. Be discerning about how and when you use finite and infinite goals.

- Where you add and create the most value should determine the role you play. Be brutally honest with yourself.

- Figure out who is your Right Client, and what is your Right Value Proposition or Right Exchange of Value. Most people get one of these wrong.

TRY THIS:

It takes effort to define your Today's Eagle. Here are some key steps to kickstarting that prioritization process:

1 Look at your calendar over the next one to four weeks. Make a list of all the activities on it.

2 Go down the list and cross off the activities that are sabotaging your Future Eagle, your desired future. Find a way to either stop doing these activities or delegate them.

3 Review the items that are serving your desired future and determine if you need to do anything differently.

4   On a new piece of paper write a list of all the things you need to start doing to serve your desired future.

5   Order the list in terms of which activity will have the biggest impact.

6   Schedule time in your calendar to start working on the one that will have the most impact on your life. When you finish that one, return to the list and schedule a second activity. Rinse and repeat until you have done everything on the list.

7   Bonus points if you schedule everything on the list. You can schedule as far out as you want. Do one activity at a time until they are all complete.

For helpful tools and resources, visit keitademming.com or scan the QR code below.

8

TODAY'S WOLF

"Your greatest danger is letting the
urgent things crowd out the important."

CHARLES E. HUMMEL

STRATEGY QUADRANT, TODAY'S WOLF

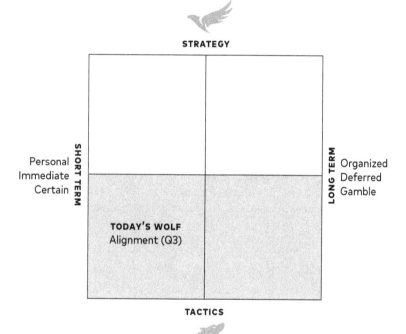

STRATEGY

Personal
Immediate
Certain

SHORT TERM

LONG TERM

Organized
Deferred
Gamble

TODAY'S WOLF
Alignment (Q3)

TACTICS

T HE POWER of the Strategy Quadrant as an orienting tool clearly shows up in the quadrant of Today's Wolf. In the previous two quadrants, Future Eagle and Today's Eagle, you are working on your business, meaning that you are planning for the short term or long term. Today's Wolf is where you work out the tactics that support and align with your long- and short-term strategies. Here you are moving from strategy to action.

The Golden Apple of Distraction

Greek mythology tells us of a young woman named Atalanta who was destined to become queen of Arcadia. However, there was an obstacle to her desired future: her parents insisted she must be married if she were to rule the land. But Atalanta had zero interest in getting hitched. Now, Atalanta was a skilled hunter and fast runner, so she struck a deal with her parents that she would only marry a man who could beat her in a foot race. Hippomenes desperately wished to marry Atalanta and so he hatched a plan to win the race. During the race, each time Atalanta would get too far ahead, he would roll a golden apple into her path to distract her and she would pause to pick it up. In the end, Hippomenes won the race by a tiny margin.

Atalanta was motivated by what was personal, immediate, and certain—golden apples. But, by picking them up, she sabotaged her Future Eagle and failed to prevent the marriage. Hippomenes's strategy was clear: to slow down Atalanta so he could win the race. He also had a clear tactic to support his strategy: to roll a golden apple in front of her each time she got too far ahead.

We all have golden apples in our lives. In the quadrant of Today's Wolf, you will need to get clear on what is getting in the way of you realizing your Future Eagle and working to avoid those things.

Working In Your Business

In the Wolf quadrants, you are working in your business as you are thinking and acting for the short term (Today's Wolf) and the long term (Future Wolf). However, in each Wolf quadrant you are working with a slightly different timeline, just as you do in Future Eagle and Today's Eagle, though the time horizons are shorter. In Today's Wolf, you are focused on the next three to fifteen months, whereas in Future Wolf you focus on fifteen months and beyond.

And remember, for many, day-to-day things are not what will help them realize their desired future, which means their Today's Wolf is not serving their Future Eagle. As I mentioned in chapter 5, this usually plays out in one of three ways:

- **Trap 1:** Your strategy and tactics never meet.

- **Trap 2:** Your strategy and tactics collide with or sabotage one another.

- **Trap 3:** You start with tactics and never examine how what you do in the short term influences a particular desired outcome in the long term.

When faced with trade-offs between immediate and future rewards, our tendency is to choose more immediate pay-offs. We sabotage our Future Eagle by choosing the golden apple. Or more realistically, we choose to go for drinks with our friends over hitting the gym, or we go along to get along instead of having the difficult conversation. Once you understand the idea that what we do in the short term needs to serve the future, you are in a far better place to develop strategies that will help you do that.

When I was doing my PhD, I met Haesun (pronounced Hey-sun) Moon, who would become a friend, colleague, and client. Although her coaching business was already successful, like many of our clients, she felt like she was making it up as she went along. She wanted to do more and make a bigger impact with her work. She decided she needed help growing her business, so she joined our Business Builder Program.

At that time, Haesun did not have a clear sense of where she wanted to be in ten years. During our program, she realized that she wanted to take her business in a new direction and a key part of that was writing a book. But when Haesun looked at her packed calendar, she could not fathom when she would find the time to write. I reminded her that unless she made a change, she would likely find herself in the same place three to five years from now. "How does your calendar reflect where you want to be three to five years from now?" I asked her. She responded, "It doesn't." Next, I asked, "What is one small thing we can do to change that?"

Eventually Haesun told her assistant, Bailey, that she was going to write every Monday and on Tuesday and Wednesday mornings. She instructed Bailey to schedule clients outside of those time slots. Inevitably a client asked Bailey to schedule an appointment during Haesun's writing time. Bailey refused and told Haesun that she would work with the client to find a time that worked for them, even if that meant they didn't connect for some time. Haesun reluctantly agreed and Bailey became part of Haesun's accountability framework. She was putting the bell on the cat by making sure that Haesun's calendar reflected what she wanted in the future. Left to her own devices, Haesun would have probably continued to make the short-term choice of not using her designated writing time to craft her desired future. But because she made that change in her calendar, and found support to make that happen, she was able to write and publish her book, *Coaching A to Z: The Extraordinary Use of Ordinary Words.*

When I was preparing to write this book, I interviewed Haesun and was delighted to learn that she attributes much of her success to our work together. What was the most important lesson for her? Learning to think and act on a much longer time horizon.

Haesun worked to ensure that her short complex tasks were in service of her desired future. Sometimes that meant she had to forgo short-term revenue for long-term potential revenue. I know how hard this may be for some people. And let me just say that I could share countless stories of people we have worked with who have given up short-term rewards and earned significant returns in the long term. Alternatively, I can share stories of people who were not willing to make changes in the short term and so they struggled to realize their desired future. In almost every case, these people are picking up golden apples.

When Haesun redesigned her calendar, she was designing her Today's Wolf. Here is what Haesun's strategy might look like:

TODAY'S EAGLE	FUTURE EAGLE
• Manage my calendar. • Develop an accountability system.	Vision: Be a thought leader in the world of coaching. Strategy: Write a compelling book on coaching.

TODAY'S WOLF	FUTURE WOLF
• Write every M/T/W morning. • Develop a plan to build my brand as a thought leader.	• Invest in the marketing of the book. • Implement a plan to build my brand as a thought leader.

Turn Your Short-Term Strategies into Supporting Activities

If you are to make your Future Eagle a reality, you must get rigorous when it comes to your supporting activities in Today's Wolf. And since we live in a complex world and cannot know for certain that a strategy or activity will work, you must think of your strategy and the activities to support it as an experiment. The purpose of experimentation is to test the validity of the strategy and the tactics. Chances are, your first attempts to marry your strategy with tactics will either not work out or, at the very least, one or both will need to be improved. Imagine yourself as a scientist who is using certain tactics to test their strategic hypothesis and the effectiveness of the tactic itself.

For example, Malika, the nurse from chapter 6, initially thought she could easily add doctors to her client roster given her connection with these health care professionals. However, when she put a plan into place to connect with them directly, it failed. At that point, she realized that she needed to adjust both her strategy (she went after different health care professionals) and her tactics (she contacted these individuals indirectly through other activities).

Avoid The Urgency-Uncertainty Trap

When you realize that you are either settling for the status quo or sabotaging your Future Eagle with what you do daily, you might find yourself struggling with time issues to resolve this. If you are reading this book, it is likely that you are opportunity rich and resource poor. When things are urgent, it often means your time is constrained and likely you make trade-offs around how you spend your time and resources.

In their book *Scarcity: Why Having Too Little Means So Much*, Sendhil Mullainathan and Eldar Shafir outline how scarcity reduces the capacity of the brain. In one study they reference, it was found that sugar cane farmers performed 25 percent better on an abstract reasoning test after harvest than before it. So, what was happening here? Simply put, scarcity affects your capacity for decision making.

Before the harvest, the farmers were experiencing scarcity. They had little money and were simply trying to survive until harvest time, so they made short-term decisions that solved their immediate problems and ignored future consequences. For example, some farmers took unfavourable loans to resolve short-term problems. The farmers focused on solving the problems right in front of them, even when it meant that in the long run they might be worse off.

It is not uncommon for our clients to express that they are reluctant to invest in the future they wish to create. Typically, they are reluctant precisely because the future is uncertain. They find it easier to invest in those things that are personal, immediate, and certain.

Many of us are caught in this urgency-uncertainty trap. You might be struggling to make payroll. You may not like your high-paying job. You may want to change careers. You might be worrying about where the next client will come from. You might be concerned about a looming deadline. All these pressures may make you feel reluctant to invest in the long term because you are struggling with the short term. You feel trapped. Your self-talk sounds like, "I just need to get through this day, this week, or this month."

As a consequence, you are caught between being unsure about making the investment in your desired future and addressing the tasks that are urgent and important but do not serve the future you wish to create. You might find it difficult to think about executing tasks, plans, or strategies that will bear fruit in the long term and free you from the urgency-uncertainty trap. And some people are so consumed by the short term that even thinking about the long term is overwhelming. I am here to say, there is a way out.

Commit to Your Transition

One of the first steps to take to exit the urgency-uncertainty trap is to commit to the reality that transitions take time. This is another way of saying, raise the level of your gaze (chapter 6) or think on a longer timeline. In effect, you are keeping one eye on the present and the other on the future.

Norm Trainor, founder of The Covenant Group, often reminds our clients that it takes two to three years to create a change. The harsh truth is that people who are seeking to transform their life or their business often need three to seven years to make that transition. When you recognize that transitions take time, and that you need to change your daily habits and routines, only then can you begin the journey to redefining performance. It is only when you have fully committed to engaging in the process that you really begin to see results. Remember, the goal is to align what we are doing in the short term (Today's Wolf) with what we want and where we want to go. The activities and tasks we do each day must be informed by our Future Eagle.

If I simplify the concept of strategy to mean the goals you want to achieve, and your tactics as the steps you need to take to get there, then the Wolf quadrants are about redefining those steps. In Today's Wolf, you are redefining those things you need to do daily, weekly, monthly, quarterly, and annually to achieve your goals. Typically, when it comes to Today's Wolf, you should be thinking along two timelines: (1) the next week to a month and (2) the next fifteen to eighteen months. Then you work to align what you are doing in these shorter timelines with the timelines of your Future Eagle.

For example, Nia was a young mother who originally got into the financial service sector because she needed to learn about money and budgeting to get her family out of debt. Once she had stabilized her own finances, she realized that she could teach others in the same situation to do so as well. The challenge was that because she was working with people who had no money, she was not making enough money. Her fifteen-month strategy was to get to a place where she could have more time to work with women who came from families with a household income of $250,000 so she could make more money for her own family. She then implemented two short-term strategies with the goal of freeing up her time:

1 She offered group classes three times a year for women in financial difficulty.

2 She created an on-demand course and charged those clients half her hourly rate for the same content and process that she used when meeting with them one on one.

Nia realized she could help these women and their families, *and* she could also make more money. She just needed to align her Today's Wolf and her supporting activities with her Future Eagle.

Start Small and Build Intentionally

When Jeff Bezos's net worth reached $163 billion, more than twice that of Warren Buffett and Bill Gates, he was asked by the *Wall Street Journal* why he was so successful. He told the *WSJ* that one of his main guidelines is that everything starts small. He explained that when he started Amazon in 1994, the company had a small number of employees. Since then Amazon has grown to become one of the largest companies in the world.

At The Covenant Group, we encourage our clients to identify three Result Priorities and three Activity Priorities that will drive revenue and their desired results. Like Bezos, we too have seen the power in starting small and building intentionally. To design your Today's Wolf, you need to take these steps to build intentionally:

1 Identify what's important to you and outline the series of steps that will be required to get you from where you are to where you want to be.

2 Identify the three results you want to achieve in the next fifteen to eighteen months. Be specific with regard to the outputs/objectives you want to attain over that time span.

3 Identify the three activities that will drive these results.

Let's see how that works in practice. We asked Jason Boudreau, the successful financial advisor in chapter 6, to identify the three Result Priorities he wanted to achieve in the next twelve months. Jason determined that he wanted to double his business within the next year, so his three Result Priorities were:

1 Generate $3,000,000 in revenue.

2 Place 30 life insurance cases with an average premium of $70,000.

3 Increase net assets under management by $40,000,000.

Next, Jason needed to develop three Activity Priorities that supported his Result Priorities.

1 Have eight meetings per week with clients in his pipeline to advance sales.

2 Meet with five new people per week who have been introduced by a client or centre of influence and engage in a Client Attraction Conversation.

3 Conduct two meetings per week with clients or centres of influence to obtain introductions.

The key was identifying the three activities that would have the greatest impact on achieving the outcomes Jason desired. These three Activity Priorities made a meaningful difference in Jason's business. He knew what he needed to do each week, each month. Additionally, he made sure that his support staff understood that his calendar needed to reflect his three Activity Priorities. In getting clear on what he needed to do day in and day out, Jason aligned his Future Eagle and Today's Eagle.

To be effective in Today's Wolf, you must get clear about what you will do in the short term. Many entrepreneurs run their business "cash on cash." They are operating in a fight-or-flight mindset, are reactive, and are focused on how they are going to cover this month's income and expense needs. That's the definition of a scarcity mindset. Others are constantly chasing the next sale, commission, or fee. Employees are caught in jobs that bring them little joy. All of them are driven by fear of failure and are too scared to make the jump that will take them to their desired future. They are surviving, rather than thriving. Their adrenal glands are working over-time, cortisol is racing through their bodies. And all of them are focused on the short term. Their actions are driven by the question: What do I need to do today, this week, or this month?

Moving from surviving to thriving starts by elevating the level of your gaze and looking out to one, three, five, and ten years or more. Then the focus becomes what you are doing in the short term that would lead to success and fulfillment, as you define it. Just remember to start small and build intentionally.

Delaying Your Future Is Expensive

Every year there are people who call The Covenant Group to express that they are thinking about joining our program, and we have a conversation with them about their problems and needs. There is a pattern to these calls in that usually they express how they are caught in a web of so-called urgent tasks that prevent them from getting to the important, strategic work of working *on* rather than *in* the business.

One individual who signed up for our coaching program, let's call him Enzi, had known for seven years that he needed to change the person in his company's administrative role. We told Enzi he had two options: he could settle for the sta-tus quo—which in Enzi's case meant sabotaging his desired future—or he could serve his desired future.

Three months later, Enzi changed his admin person, and within twelve months he had grown the business by 30 per-cent. Imagine how he might have grown the business if he had changed that admin person seven years earlier! Enzi was always reluctant to make the change because it was going to cost him. But what he lost in not making the change was 30 percent growth over a seven-year period.

To be effective in Today's Wolf, you must be clear about the tasks you will perform each day that move you from a mind-set of surviving to thriving. When you are doing work that is rewarding intellectually, emotionally, and financially, it has a profound impact on the fulfillment you experience in every area of your life.

In the following chapter, I'll explore the quadrant of Future Wolf, those things that are tactical and long term. The Future Wolf addresses the structure, systems, and processes you will need to put in place to realize your desired future.

REFLECTION POINTS

- Ignore the golden apples of distraction, the things that are not in service of your desired future.

- Make a distinction between two timelines: what you need to implement in the next three to fifteen months and what you need to implement in fifteen months and beyond.

- Ensure that your tactics are in service of your strategy.

- Design your day to be in service of the future you want.

- Keep asking the alignment question: Is this action I am about to take in radical service of the future I desire?

- Remember that transitions can take anywhere from one to seven years.

- Start small and take the time to build out your three Activity and Result Priorities.

TRY THIS:

1 We judge ourselves by our intentions. Others judge us based on our actions. Take some time to think of something you have intended to do but have not yet started. What is one small thing you can do to get started on those actions?

2 Be brutally honest with yourself. Which of the following statements best describes where you find yourself today?

- I am settling for a future I do not desire.
- I am sabotaging my desired future.
- I am radically serving my desired future.

9

FUTURE
WOLF

"Strategy is simply resource allocation.
When you strip away all the noise,
that's what it comes down to."

JACK WELCH

STRATEGY QUADRANT, FUTURE WOLF

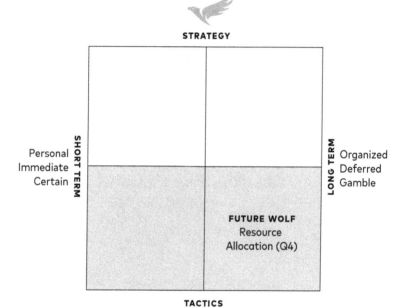

STRATEGY

Personal
Immediate
Certain

SHORT TERM

LONG TERM

Organized
Deferred
Gamble

FUTURE WOLF
Resource
Allocation (Q4)

TACTICS

N THE previous chapter, I described the purpose of diving into Today's Wolf in the Strategy Quadrant as the way to help you become grounded, action-oriented, and disciplined in your execution and management of complex tasks in the short term. The Future Wolf quadrant focuses on those things that are long term and tactical. Here you are going to focus on long-term complex tasks and the allocation of your resources to the systems and processes that you need to achieve your desired future.

In Today's Wolf, you are working within a timeline of three to eighteen months. In Future Wolf, you will shift your focus to eighteen months and beyond. These are the three questions that are essential to building out your Future Wolf:

1   What role do you want to play?

2   How big do you want your company to be?

3   What is the structure required to achieve your desired future?

The last of these questions is the most important for Future Wolf, but to get there you need to answer the first two. Nailah will serve as our example of the journey to building out the Future Wolf. As you'll see, the journey through the Future Wolf quadrant is also dependent on navigating both Future Eagle and Today's Eagle as well as Today's Wolf.

Moving from Income Producer to Business Builder

Nailah was a successful entrepreneur who built her business based on her charisma and status as a former professional soccer player. After playing and coaching professional athletes for eleven years, she returned to her hometown to build a design and branding firm, which was an immediate success. In just three years, her income exceeded $500,000.

TODAY'S EAGLE

- Focus on building relationships while coaching her team to take over roles she would no longer be doing.
- Disentangle marketing, sales, and client service.
- Implement a Client Relationship Management system.
- Build a cash reserve.

FUTURE EAGLE

Vision:
Grow firm into a nationwide organization that serves athletes and the brands they engage with.

Strategy:
- Focus on creating brand wealth for clients through top-notch design.
- Keep the company small and nimble while building out an ecosystem of trusted contractors and vendors.

TODAY'S WOLF

- Design her day so she is focused on relationship building.
- Map out a plan for who she is going to hire and when.
- Map out a plan for what technology she would implement and when.
- Determine which service would be insourced and which would be outsourced.

FUTURE WOLF

- Map out who she will need to hire and when over the next three to five years.
- Map out what technology she will need and when over the next five years.
- Build in checks and balances to ensure quality and continuous improvement.

Nailah had succeeded at becoming an income producer. She was replacing income earned by working for someone else with income earned through her own efforts. But Nailah wanted more. She wanted to grow her firm into a nationwide organization that served athletes and the brands they engage with. This was her Future Eagle.

Until that point, growth had come naturally to Nailah's business. Like many talented people, Nailah was able to leverage her unique capabilities to grow her business. But she could only do so much. She was front and centre in the business activities and needed to begin to free up her time to work on the business rather than in it. She was aware that her success going forward required a different approach. She needed to become a Business Builder. And there are two key lessons that entrepreneurs like Nailah need to learn:

1 Your business does not grow in a linear progression.
2 Successful businesses are built on replicable processes.

The growth of most businesses tends to follow a series of "S" curves with breakpoints, or ceilings of complexity, that determine whether they will evolve to the next level. Each curve consists of:

- an initial stage of formation or building the base for growth
- a second stage of significant growth
- a final stage of slowing growth and eventual plateauing

The peak of the "S" curve is the breakpoint. At this point, future growth requires a new approach and the formation of a new "S" curve. Nailah needed to move to a new curve. She had leveraged her strengths and competencies to get where she was but, like many entrepreneurs, she got stuck. Her vision required a new structure. She needed to build systems and processes that would support her desired future.

A large part of our work at The Covenant Group involves working with our clients to develop the systems and processes that will drive revenue and measurable results. Systems and processes provide the framework for running the business. We define a system as a "set of detailed methods, procedures, and routines created to carry out a specific activity, perform a duty or solve a problem." A system is a bundling of processes. A process is a pattern or method that is distinguishable, repeatable, and transferable. Nailah needed to focus on playing the infinite game by leveraging people, capital, and technology. She would build the structure and the structure would build the business.

Playing the Infinite Game

Nailah's initial success in business was based upon playing a finite game. When you leverage your unique strengths, you are playing a finite game. The success of the business or practice is dependent upon leveraging the time, energy, creativity, and intelligence of the principal or founder. Nailah needed to start playing a different game. She began to realize that one person, no matter how talented, can bring only so much to grow the business, and at some point, growth stalls. To build the business she envisioned, Nailah had to move to playing an infinite game.

In an infinite game, the objective is to leverage not only your unique ability but also the unique capabilities of all the people inside and outside your organization to help grow the business. To take her business to the next level, Nailah had to make the transition from "player" to "player/coach."

Now that she needed to play an infinite game, as a player/coach Nailah had a dual responsibility. She was a star player in the business, but also a coach who was responsible for the overall success of the team. The company could no longer be about her and her performance.

Nailah's gift was her ability to earn the trust of her clients. When she was playing a finite game, Nailah worked with two assistants whose responsibility it was to ensure that she could focus on what she did best—building relationships by connecting with clients and prospects. Her two support people were charged with ensuring that Nailah worked at the highest level of her capability.

Nailah realized that if she wanted to build a multimillion-dollar business, she would have to attract other designers. In addition, she would need qualified staff that could perform specialized functions, such as a brand strategist and a marketing coordinator or account manager. She could no longer afford the luxury of solely working with assistants. Instead, she needed an organizational structure with defined roles, role relationships, accountabilities, and authority for each person on the team. Nailah needed to define her business, set objectives, and develop the strategies for building a multimillion-dollar enterprise.

Initially, within her Today's Wolf, Nailah was focused on hiring an account manager and designer so that she was no longer caught up in the service delivery of the work. She needed to work on disentangling marketing, sales, and client service. In the short term, she was going to focus on finding people who could handle client service, hence the search for an account manager and designer. Next, in her Future Wolf, Nailah needed to plan further out.

She knew that given her projected growth she would need to hire an additional account manager and designer at around the twelve-month mark. She also wanted to build cash in the business to reduce her concerns around managing expenses. And also she needed to acquire a Client Relationship

Management system (CRM). Since she wanted to grow a nationwide company, she decided to find an IT company that could support a remote team—she did not want to figure out why files were not syncing or why she was not receiving a client's email. Finally, she wanted to outsource the bookkeeping since she hated doing it and found tax season stressful.

Nailah could not possibly do all these projects at the same time, but she knew that each of these changes would be crucial to building the design firm of her dreams. In and among all that growth, she needed to establish what role she wanted to play, where she brought the most value.

What Role Do You Want to Play?

Like many of the people we work with, Nailah was a facing a paradox. She needed to become accountable for fewer areas in her business, while still being responsible for everything. This meant she needed to delegate to people, capital, and technology. To optimize her performance, she had to do less and delegate accountability to others. As the saying goes, "Do what you are best at and delegate the rest."

Where most people start in answering this question is to think about what they like doing or want to do. Unfortunately, the things you like doing are not always the things that will bring you the most success. Instead, focus on the things you do better than anyone else in your organization. Ask yourself, What do I do that undoubtedly adds the most value? If you can answer this question objectively, you are well on your way to defining the role you want to play and starting your journey of redefining your performance.

Nassor, the CEO who demoted himself to head of marketing, wanted to work where he added the most value to the company. Similarly, Nailah realized she added the most value in developing strategy, bringing on new clients, and identifying prospects. She needed to focus on those three things and build a team or ecosystem around her so she could work at the highest level of her capability. She then needed to answer the next question: How big did she want her business to become?

How Big Do You Want to Be?

At The Covenant Group, we have had the privilege of interacting with many incredible entrepreneurs. One example is David Falk, a pre-eminent sports agent in North America. He is known as the person responsible for the Air Jordan brand, a brand that has generated $5 billion in revenue over three decades. One of the stories David shares is of his own approach in answering the question, How big do you want to become?

Prior to building his own company, David helped build a 900-person athlete management company, but he did not enjoy working in such a large organization. Like the lawyer Omari, he realized that quality over quantity was key. It was easier to work with an athlete who was making $15-$30 million than with one making $5-$10 million. When he ventured out to start his own company, he narrowed his focus and worked with fewer athletes, who made more money. When he sold his company, it was worth more than the 900-person company that he left, with a fraction of the client base.

"How big do you want to become?" is a strategic question with tactical implications. Tactically, it helps you understand the size and structure of the organization you will need to support the role you want to play. And having a good sense of the growth you wish to achieve informs the systems and processes you will need to support that organization.

There is nothing wrong with wanting to have a big company. But if you do, make sure you want it for the right reasons. Too often, businesspeople decide they want a big company because they have something to prove to themselves and others. Many of them believe that bigger is better, and they define their success based on the size of their business. They also say things like, "My dad (or friend) built a big company, and I want to do the same."

This can be dangerous territory. When you develop your strategy and tactics from a place of ego, it rarely ends well. Jim Collins, author of *Good to Great*, says, "A company should limit its growth based on its ability to attract the right people." I would add: as long as that growth helps it achieve its vision and mission. Many of the people we have worked with at The Covenant Group wanted to create a big company, but when they started to plan out what is required to grow and manage one, they often came to appreciate that small can be beautiful.

When you are thinking about how big you want to become, consider these questions:

- How many employees do you want to manage?
- How many clients do you want to have?
- How many offices do you want to have?
- How much revenue do you want to generate?
- How many products do you want to manage?

When Nailah considered these questions, she decided she wanted a company with no more than fifteen people on payroll. That meant she needed to outsource functions and build an ecosystem of contract vendors to create the company that was right for her. Now she was ready to answer the final question: What is the structure, or requisite organization, required to achieve your desired future? What would you need?

Ask yourself,
What do I do that
undoubtedly adds
the most value?

What Structure Do You Need?

In the Future Wolf quadrant, you want to focus on building out the required organization to suit your needs. Here, you are designing the structure of the organization you wish to create. The design should focus on identifying the most important activities that help you make your desired future a reality. Since both quadrants of the Wolf zone are primarily about execution and implementation, you will focus on answering:

1   What is the structure you will need to implement your Future Eagle?

2   What are the systems and processes you will need to put in place to support your Future Eagle?

3   What people, capital, and technology will you need?

But building out the Future Wolf is not about having a plan; it's about having a planning process. Let me show you how that works.

When Nailah thought about her future company, she understood that there could be other people in her ecosystem, like bookkeepers, IT support, photographers, and other freelance professionals. However, she did not want a company that was too big. She thought she could grow the company by adding two people in the first year, five in the second year, and eight in the third year. These roles would include admin support, project managers, designers, account managers, and a production manager to lead the video content she thought she would need.

Given her company's rate of growth, she knew she wanted her CRM in place by the end of the second year. She decided that her fourth hire would be a project manager to implement the CRM system. She wanted someone who could integrate the CRM with the workflow of the office and also take some of the workload off the account managers and admin support.

With these benchmarks established, Nailah mapped out her requisite organizational development over the next three to five years. Here's how that map looked from the perspective of Nailah's Today's Wolf and Future Wolf:

TODAY'S WOLF (NEXT 15–18 MONTHS)

Hire designer	Hire account manager and start building a cash reserve	Hire project manager and source bookkeeper

FUTURE WOLF (18 MONTHS AND BEYOND)

Hire admin support, account manager, and designer. Start implementing CRM	Source managed IT service. Hire project manager	Standardize freelancer process and build the network	Hire production manager

For Nailah, each block represented a project, or a hunt, as she liked to call it because wolves hunt in packs. Mapping out her Future Wolf broke things down for Nailah and eased her sense of overwhelm.

As it happened, Nailah needed to hire some people sooner than she thought and to delay other hires, but having a rough plan made it easier for her to shuffle things around. She knew she did not have to think about some hunts for another three to four months, which freed up her headspace. Although it was important for Nailah that she took on no more than three major hunts at the same time, she always knew which ones to focus on. And she knew that once she completed a specific hunt, she could move on to the next.

NAILAH'S EFFORTS are a great example of setting the stage for planning and plotting a Future Wolf. She was able to clearly outline and focus on those things that were procedural and she was able to articulate her requisite organization. In the next chapter, I will show you what each quadrant looked like for Nailah.

REFLECTION POINTS

- When your growth is stuck, it is time to redefine your performance.

- Playing the infinite game is another form of playing the long game. When you play the infinite game you leverage the time, energy, creativity, and intelligence of others.

- Determine the right structure for your business by clarifying the role you want to play and how big you want to become.

- Successful businesses are built on replicable processes.

- A key part of playing at the highest level of your capability is having well-defined systems and processes.

- The more you refine the systems and processes of your business, the more likely you are to play at the highest level of your capability.

TRY THIS:

In your work, there are three questions you will need to answer:

1 What role do you want to play?
2 How big do you want to become?
3 What is the required or requisite organization?

Take some time to write out the answers to these questions and share them with trusted people in your circle. Get feedback and iterate on the answers.

For helpful tools and resources, visit keitademming.com or scan the QR code below.

10

WHEN EAGLES AND WOLVES WORK TOGETHER

"One's destination is never a place, but rather a new way of looking at things."

HENRY MILLER

T HROUGHOUT THIS BOOK I have outlined the Strategy Quadrant and provided you with examples of how some people have navigated its sub-quadrants. In this chapter, I will return to Nailah as an example of how you bring the Strategy Quadrant together. In the final section of the chapter, I will walk you through how to think about and apply the Strategy Quadrant to your own life.

Nailah found herself in a situation common with many entrepreneurs: she needed to redefine her business if she wanted to grow it. Starting with her Future Eagle, she needed to define where she wanted to go and then align her strategies and tactics with that destination in mind.

Q1: Future Eagle (long-term strategy and vision) → Desired Future

The Future Eagle quadrant is all about articulating your desired future. Where do you want to be in five or ten years? Nailah's vision was to build a multimillion-dollar design firm to serve athletes. Her key strategy to building the company was to create brand wealth for athletes and entertainers through top-notch design and marketing. She wanted to keep the company small, with no more than fifteen people on payroll, so her plan was to build an ecosystem of contractors, vendors, and outsourced functions to help her stay agile. She got clear on her revenue goals and the number of clients she needed to meet those goals.

Q2: Today's Eagle (short-term strategy) → Prioritizing

Nailah needed to prioritize what she was going to start doing, stop doing, and continue doing. For her plan to work, she needed to slowly transition some of the many tasks on her plate to other people so she could work at the highest level of her capability—building relationships with potential clients. In this quadrant, Nailah's key strategies were to disentangle marketing, sales, and service, and implement a Client Relationship Management system to help the team work more effectively. Finally, she began building a cash reserve to ease her anxiety with respect to meeting the obligations and demands of a growing business. Nailah knew that she had a habit of making poor decisions when cashflow was tight. So, for her, building a cash reserve was a way of improving her own decision making.

Q3: Today's Wolf (short-term tactics) → Alignment

In this quadrant the focus is on alignment: making sure that the things you do in the short term are in radical service of your desired future. In this quadrant you clarify what jobs need to be done and how you are going to do them. Here Nailah focused on designing her day and week so she could be laser-focused on the things that would help her realize her desired future. Over a two-year period, she mapped out who she was going to hire and when, when she would implement the software she thought she needed, and when she would outsource various activities. She also clarified her short-term revenue goals and made sure she was having the appropriate number of meetings to meet her goals. All the while, she focused on aligning what she was doing each day with the future she envisioned.

Q4: Future Wolf (long-term tactics) → Resource Allocation

The Future Wolf quadrant is an extension of Today's Wolf. It is where you determine how and when you will allocate resources. In this quadrant, Nailah mapped out the resources, people, systems, and processes she thought she would need over the next three years. This gave her the time and space to prepare and plan how she would execute. She was also able to add in buffers for the inevitable unexpected events.

Become an Iterative Thinker

One of my clients told me he loved how the Strategy Quadrant asked him to reconsider his future on a regular basis. He found the idea of moving from linear thinking to iterative thinking extremely valuable and liked to think of the quadrant as using loops.

The first time you go through the Strategy Quadrant, you start with the Future Eagle. Once you have articulated your Future Eagle, you may choose to navigate the quadrant in whatever way makes sense to you. So, from Future Eagle you can choose to move to either Today's Eagle or Today's Wolf. Once in a while you will go to your Future Wolf. The idea is that you should iterate by continually reviewing each quadrant, but always using the Future Eagle as your compass or guide.

Those steps could look something like:

- Step 1: Future Eagle
- Step 2: Today's Eagle
- Step 3: Today's Wolf
- Step 4: Future Wolf
- Step 5: Return to the Future Eagle
- Step 6: You choose

The quadrant is meant to transform your strategy planning into an iterative process. For example, suppose you and your partner have decided to use it to plan your retirement. Whenever one of you is about to make a decision, you use the quadrant as your tool for making the best one. You ask yourself, How does this action serve our Future Eagle? That action might be buying a new car, changing jobs, sending your kids to private school, going for dinner with a friend, or exercising. But the question only makes sense if you have taken the time to first articulate your Future Eagle. Once you do, your short-term decisions are always framed in the context of your long-term goals.

Keep in mind that strategy is an ongoing conversation. So the goals are dynamic and continually evolve as new opportunities and challenges present themselves. The Strategy

Quadrant is a planning process, not a journey with a beginning and an end. Your goal is not to complete each quadrant but to navigate them on an ongoing basis with the goal of keeping your eye on the future and connecting it to your present situation.

THE STRATEGY QUADRANT is a simple tool that can be remarkably effective in helping you realize the future you desire. In the next chapter, I'll highlight some of the major insights that have come out of using the Strategy Quadrant with our clients.

REFLECTION POINTS

- Your strategy development is an iterative process. The Strategy Quadrant is your tool for keeping that top-of-mind.

- The Future Eagle is the anchor to which you continually return as you navigate the Strategy Quadrant.

- There is no right way or only way to navigate the Strategy Quadrant.

- The quadrant is your tool to help you determine if this next action puts you in a better position.

- The first time you complete the Strategy Quadrant, it is just a draft. Your task is to test your strategic hypothesis and assumptions you made as you created the quadrant.

TRY THIS:

Draw a first draft of the Strategy Quadrant. (To download templates and more resources visit keitademming.com.)

Once you have completed your first draft, share it with trusted people in your circle. Get feedback and update or revise the answers.

11

INSIGHTS FROM THE STRATEGY QUADRANT

"Strategy is not the consequence of
planning, but the opposite: its starting point."

HENRY MINTZBERG

W HEN WE FIRST introduced the Strategy Quadrant to our clients at The Covenant Group, we were delighted to see how well it resonated with them. Many clients found creative ways of applying the quadrant in their daily lives. One client even divided all his time into Eagle and Wolf activities. He specified times when he would work on strategy and when he would work on tactics, always confirming that the two were aligned. Now that you understand how the Strategy Quadrant works, I hope you have a better understanding of what it means to bell the cat— to close the gap between strategy and tactics.

In this chapter, I'd like to highlight eight insights that we have gleaned from how people have applied the Strategy Quadrant to their lives and businesses. But first it's important to acknowledge that all models are imperfect, incomplete, and can be improved. The Strategy Quadrant is no different. Use the tool appropriately because it is not one-size-fits-all and won't solve all your problems.

1. The Strategy Quadrant makes you comfortable with iterative thinking

Too many people think of their strategy as static and not as a temporary holding position. When your assumptions regarding your strategy change, so too should your strategy. The key question in thinking about strategy is the "What must be true?" question. Once you have gone through the quadrant, you need to ask, What is still true or what still needs to be true? When you stop asking the questions, you've ended the conversation. Keep talking and after a while you'll become comfortable with iterative thinking—it's a game changer—and you'll find yourself more agile when it comes to clarifying your Future Eagle.

2. The Strategy Quadrant kicks you out of autopilot

Remember the story of the fly in the urinal? The placement of a fly was designed to help kick men out of autopilot and get them to focus on what they are doing. When you keep the Strategy Quadrant top-of-mind, you are continually reminded to align your short-term activities with the future you wish to create.

One of my clients posted a copy of his Strategy Quadrant next to his computer to remind him to spend the day in service of his desired future. Another client has a note in his bathroom that says, Did you serve your Future Eagle today?

3. The Strategy Quadrant helps you distinguish between urgent and important

When people map their activities onto the Strategy Quadrant, it allows them to discern between activities that are urgent and those that are important. Our brains are often captured by urgent things. Your task is to discern which tasks are urgent or important while still creating time for those things that are less so. When you focus on the Future Eagle, it improves your chances of focusing on those things that are truly important.

Our client Marcus Mackay, the personal trainer who founded a successful company, has implemented a guideline to always work on "money later" tasks first. The concept is that "money later" tasks are those that will generate revenue in the future, whereas "money today" tasks generate money in the short term.

When you use the Strategy Quadrant to prioritize those things that are important and not urgent, it helps level the playing field between your future self and present self. When you take the time to design your present self, you increase your chances of meeting your future desired self. Focusing on serving your Future Eagle reminds you to make good investments in your future self, today.

4. The Strategy Quadrant helps you identify and implement simple guidelines

Our clients have reported that it is much easier to establish simple guidelines when they know their Future Eagle. The guidelines help them take action on those things that are in service of their desired future. The rules cue them on when to start doing things, and when to stop or continue doing other things.

My favourite example of this is a study of small-business owners in the Dominican Republic who were given financial literacy training. The experimenters took two approaches to training study participants. One was a traditional approach that taught business owners the fundamentals of financial literacy. The second approach taught simple guidelines. For example, rather than teaching the notion of working capital management, participants were taught a few simple guidelines: assign yourself a monthly wage, pay yourself at the start of the week, and never take money out of the business. This guideline helped small-business owners know how profitable they were without understanding working capital. The advantage of these simple guidelines was that business owners could follow the simple rules without needing to fully understand the complex reasons why they are important. The researchers found that the group that was taught simple guidelines significantly outperformed those who were taught with the traditional approach.

5. You can't be a lone wolf in the Strategy Quadrant

In the Strategy Quadrant, the Wolf zones are where you focus on implementation and execution. Like humans, wolves are social animals. They seek companionship, and while they may go through periods of solitude, they are not interested in a lifetime of it. Wolves want to be part of a pack, a community. When wolves strike out on their own, they do it to build a new community.

One of our clients thought of himself as a lone wolf. He did not want or think he needed anyone in his pack. After working through the Strategy Quadrant, he realized that to thrive he needed to recruit a team he could depend on. He needed his own wolf pack to help him execute his vision. It wasn't that he worked best alone, it was that he hadn't found the right people.

Society, especially Western society, has sold us the lie of the lone wolf. We are social animals and need others to thrive. Take the time to find your people. And make sure they are the right people because you do not want any weak wolves.

6. The Strategy Quadrant is a team builder

When teams problem-solve together, they create bonds. Teams working through the Strategy Quadrant often build rapport that creates a sense of shared experience within teams and across companies.

We have seen how working with the Strategy Quadrant in quarterly meetings can motivate and energize teams, whereas strategy planning events are usually one-day performances that bring teams together to build a report that often ends up sitting on the shelf.

As well, most workshops do a poor job of transferring any learning from the session into the workplace. In contrast, using the Strategy Quadrant as a guide helps bring the learning and implementation into the organization because it makes strategy and tactics more accessible. Conversation around the Strategy Quadrant helps build the rapport required to achieve great things together. The work of building out the Strategy Quadrant helps teams integrate strategy in all aspects of their work so that they feel ownership of both the process and the outcome.

7. The Strategy Quadrant helps you find abundance

Scarcity can come in many forms other than money. It can show up as a scarcity of time, emotions, or resources. All of these types of scarcity hijack our brains into focusing on solving problems in front of us. But planning for the future requires bandwidth. When you have no bandwidth it's hard to think about and act in alignment with the future you wish to create.

If you can find ways to create an abundance of time, resources, or emotional capacity, it can have a huge impact on the kinds of decisions you make. For example, for most solopreneurs, the best thing they can do to create time and resource abundance is to hire an assistant. One of the best ways to create abundance is to design your environment to help you stay focused on the things you want to attain in your life.

8. The Strategy Quadrant inspires you to consider new approaches

Another way to create abundance in your life is to add slack to your system. For people who are at or near capacity, this might seem ludicrous. But one example of how it can work is provided by the case of St. John's Regional Health Center.

Christine Dempsey, vice president of perioperative services, was attending a learning session of patient flow management when she was introduced to a novel idea for solving the hospital's many problems. Christine had found that unplanned or emergency surgeries were relatively predictable, but they always left the hospital personnel scrambling. The novel idea was to leave two beds open for these unscheduled yet predictable surgeries. After implementing this radical idea, the hospital saw a range of improvements, including an all-time low in operating room overtime and improved staff and patient satisfaction.

I often share this story with clients as a way of helping them understand that they have to redefine their Today's Wolf if they are to redefine their future. Sometimes you will need to do things that may not work, will not give you results immediately, or seem hard. Sometimes you may need to do things that cost you in the short term but may give you the results you seek in the long term.

Are You Prepared to Meet Your Future Self?

At one time in my life I did a lot of running. I am also a people watcher and one of the things I like to watch is the end of a running race. I often see that there are generally two types of people at the end of a 10K race or marathon. There are those who are smiling and laughing and look like they are ready to run the race again. The second kind are those who are often lying on the ground and are happy the race is over. These people might be asking themselves, Why did I sign up for this awful race? There are many reasons why people have these two different experiences. The most fundamental reason can be found in how they prepared for the race.

Those people who followed some kind of training plan and stuck to it are likely the ones smiling and laughing at the end of the race. Those who were less prepared are likely those who are hating their life choices at the end of the race. Life and work are similar. At the end of the day, some of us are ready to do it again. Others, unfortunately, are happy that it is over.

You will one day meet your future self. But right now that future self is a stranger. What separates those who are smiling at the finish line from those who are happy the race is over is that those who are smiling are doing so because they met their future desired self. They met the person they wanted to become. Our challenge in life is creating the conditions to meet not just our future self, but also our future desired self—the person we want to be, not the person we randomly end up being. Using the Strategy Quadrant is a process of creating alignment between the person you are today and the person you wish to become. People can get stuck in any of the quadrants. If, however, you use the quadrants consistently and effectively, you are more likely to meet your goals and objectives.

Remember you are not putting together a bike. You are not working on a machine. You are navigating a complex world and what you are doing is likely closer to raising a child. In a complex world, better conversations lead to better outcomes. The quadrant is an approach to having a better conversation with yourself, your inner circle, and the wider world of your business about strategy and tactics.

Over time I have seen that people tend to be either tactical or strategic. Sadly, most people also tend to make tactical decisions devoid of strategy. Unfortunately, when they seek help, they are told to focus on things like motivation, self-control, willpower, and self-denial. This usually implies that the reason you are not successful is that you are the problem. Although that may be true sometimes, for many of us the challenge is often that our strategy and tactics are misaligned.

On the road to success, we are constantly trading between strategy and tactics. But too many of us allow tactics to dominate our daily decisions. If you are to achieve your goals, your tactics need to be informed by your strategy, and that involves three things:

- thinking on a longer time span
- shapeshifting between the Eagle and Wolf mindsets
- doing the most important thing first and making it a priority

Thinking on a longer time span means prioritizing your Future Eagle. As a reminder, the single biggest differentiator between high performers and average ones is the time frame in which they think and plan. When you are able to move between the Eagle and Wolf, it sets you up for implementing a strategy that is integrated and coherent. When you prioritize the things that are organized, deferred, and a gamble, you prioritize the future you wish to create.

Here is the ultimate takeaway from the Strategy Quadrant: you will pay for your future no matter what you do. Why not pay for the future you want?

12

MOVING FROM FAMILIARITY TO MASTERY

"We fail to realize that
mastery is not about perfection.
It's about a process, a journey."

GEORGE LEONARD

O YOU recall a time when a well-prepared presentation had you nodding and thinking, "I get that"—but when you try to share the content with a colleague or friend, you realize that you don't know it as well as you thought? That moment is usually a sign that you are familiar with the content but have not mastered it.

As an educator, much of my work has focused on how we foster transformational learning environments. In my work at The Covenant Group, I have often observed people confusing familiarity and mastery. When I went back to the research on how we foster high-performance environments, it was clear: people are terrible at judging their own learning.

BEGINNER TO MASTERY

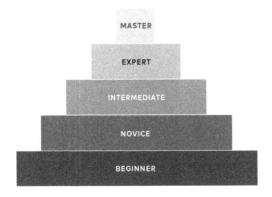

Research by Michael Kardas and Ed O'Brien in 2018 found that the more people watch others perform a task, the more confident they are in their own ability to perform that task. We overestimate our competence simply by watching a video. It may seem obvious that watching someone perform a task won't improve performance, but your brain convinces you otherwise after having observed it being performed several times. These mental hijacks steer you toward confounding familiarity with mastery.

These cognitive traps are called the "illusion of mastery" and the "familiarity illusion." This simply means you are under the illusion that you have mastered something when you are merely familiar with it. High performers work to ensure that they are not just familiar with the content, but have also mastered it.

You do not master content by reading books or listening to presentations, gurus, or coaches. To master content, you need to apply, refine, and integrate the learning into your life and work. Mastery requires a structured approach to learning. The challenge is overcoming your blind spots. I want you to come up with a plan for putting the Strategy Quadrant into action so you can move from familiarity to mastery. In my experience, high performers explicitly work to articulate their intentions, refine processes, and clearly measure their successes to move from familiarity to mastery.

For example, one of the processes we teach is called the Client Attraction Conversation. It is the initial conversation you have in a sales process. Most people who work in sales have not taken the time to master their Client Attraction Conversation. They go into each conversation making it up as they go along. Surprisingly, this works for them until they begin to get serious about mastering their sales process.

I had one client who was reasonably successful, but she also felt like she was faking her way to success. I introduced her to the idea of standardized customization. This means you have a standard approach that produces an outcome that is customized for your client. We helped her standardize her Client Attraction Conversation so that she knew exactly how she should approach every sales conversation. As a result, she found she was making sales much faster. She needed fewer meetings to close a sale and got very good at qualifying prospects.

A key differentiator of masters is that they learn to spot patterns. She now knew which questions to ask to qualify her leads. In mastering her Client Attraction Conversation, she made her sales process easier and faster.

Coaching and Peer Groups

We all have blind spots, and having someone give us feedback can be invaluable. One of the best ways to start serving your Future Eagle is through coaching and peer-to-peer groups. Coaching and peer groups not only provide you with accountability, but also help you know that you are not alone. Coaches and peers can provide you with perspective on your perspective. They help you apply, refine, and integrate your learning. An important role of a coach is to know when to support and when to challenge.

For example, I worked with an entrepreneur who never asked for introductions from his colleagues and peers. After I guided him through the process, he started to ask for introductions, but he was convinced he could get only three introductions a month. I challenged him to aim for six. To our pleasure, at the end of the month he had asked for introductions with ten people in his network. Not only did he find additional relationships, but these introductions also added tremendous value to his bottom line. As the introductions multiplied, and he became more confident, eventually he found himself with more business than he could handle. Now he regularly aims for ten introductions a month.

Your coaching can be formal or informal. Whatever path you choose, we hope that you lean into the ideas presented in this book and find your pack. So many of us have been taught to believe that success is all about self-control, willpower, and self-denial. More and more, we are learning that we are much better off building systems and structures that help us achieve our goals and saying no to what gets in the way.

BY NOW, at the end of this book, you might be wondering which mindset in the quadrant is more important, the Eagle or the Wolf. Just as no one argues if breathing in is more important than breathing out, the answer is neither. Learn to master the domains of both the Eagle and the Wolf. Each of us is naturally stronger in one than the other, but when you can build your team with the right balance of Eagles and Wolves, it can be transformative.

Now go and change the course of your river.

ACKNOWLEDGEMENTS

HAVE ALWAYS believed that it takes a village to accomplish meaningful and useful things. This book and many of the ideas in it would not have been possible without my thought partner and mentor, Norm Trainor. Many of the ideas come from the years of experience he has accumulated as an educator and coach. It has been a privilege to learn under his mentorship and although I have framed many of the ideas in the book, it is his years of sharing wisdom that have helped move it from a theoretical academic book to a practical and useful one.

The team at The Covenant Group has been nothing but supportive of the efforts to make this book possible, and I want to thank John Donnelly, Jacobo Fraile, and Candice Greenidge. I would also like to thank Dean Harder, a client and associate with The Covenant Group.

It may seem obvious to thank my wife, Shauna, but to have someone believe in your dreams more than you do is incredibly inspiring. To have someone close to you slay all the doubt monsters on your behalf is something special and I want to thank her for believing in my dream and having the conviction to support me in making it a reality. The combination of support and challenge she has shown during this journey has meant the world to me. For example, although she banned me from reading books until I finished writing this one, she also encouraged me to develop a writing schedule so she could create the space for me to write. Not all people have this kind of supportive partner, and I am grateful that I have her in my corner.

I would like to acknowledge my mentor and former professor Ed O'Sullivan and his wife, Eimear O'Neill. Ed passed away the year I was writing this book, so I am just going to write directly to him here.

Dear Ed,

Although you will never get to read it, you instructed me to write this book so many years ago. We did it, my friend. We wrote the book that we talked about at your farm. Hope to see you soon, wherever your spirit is.

Eimear has been equally supportive, opening up her empty apartment to provide me with space to write.

I want to thank my editor, Sarah Brohman, to whom I am deeply grateful for helping me turn my awful first draft into the final version of this book. Sarah pushed me to write things I did not want to write but have only served to make the book better. She also helped me take out things that were not serving you, the reader. She was the perfect editor for this book.

I am grateful to the team at Page Two. Trena White, Adrineh Der-Boghossian, and Chris Brandt have all been passionate, dedicated, and committed to helping me write the best book possible.

I am also grateful for the support of a good friend, Franziska Beeler, who really encouraged me to write this book in the early days. We met many nights to talk about this when it was simply an idea. When I did finally finish the book, Franziska provided some very thoughtful suggestions and ideas that made this book better.

While I was writing this book, Madeleine Féquière, the Canadian Consul General in Chicago, became a mentor of mine. There are two pieces of advice she gave me: First, put yourself in places where you are fearful: you will learn the most there. Second, tell people that you are a high school dropout. It is part of your story and who you are. This lesson taught me to show up as myself in this book. It helped me write a book where I am not pretending to be someone else. This book is fully me and you can thank Madeleine Féquière for that.

There are many people I have crossed paths with who deserve acknowledgement in this book. For example, Chuck Marohn, founder and president of Strong Towns, once asked me on a podcast: If you were to write a book, what would it be about? His question planted a seed. Similarly, Sharon Avery, president and CEO of Toronto Foundation, told me once, "Keita, you need to write a book. It doesn't matter what it is about, just write a book." David Burkus, the author of five best-selling books and one of the world's leading business thinkers, in a brief conversation also helped me see that I too could be an author as part of my work as an educator.

There have been many people like this who have inspired me to write my first book. To all the people who, when I shared that I was writing a book, simply said something to the effect of "that is awesome," I want to thank you for cheering for me from the sidelines. I see you and say thank you: Shauna Trainor, Doug Sharpe, Paloma Holmes, Jessicca Hawkins, Dennis Yanke, Tom Grochmal, Jessie-Lynn MacDonald, Isobel Stevenson, Kristina Riis, Richard Demming, Dennise Demming, Halalea Nugent, and Alex Heron.

Finally, as a high school dropout and someone who was diagnosed as being dyslexic, I have had a lot of people dismiss me or give up on me. I acknowledge me, Keita Demming, for my dedication and determination to make this book a reality. For all the late nights writing and wrestling with this book.

For all the times I decided not to watch television or go out with friends. And for all the times I chose to go to bed so I could wake up and write. This is me committing to a lifetime of educating and coaching to help others create the lives they dream of.

NOTES

Chapter 1

Haesun, who escaped the "tyranny of the urgent": Charles E. Hummel, *Tyranny of the Urgent* (Westmount, IL: IVP Booklets, 1994).

Chapter 2

54 percent of North Americans do not have a will: Jeffrey M. Jones, "How Many Americans Have a Will?" Gallup, June 23, 2021, news.gallup.com/poll/351500/how-many-americans-have-will.aspx.

scientific management "may well be the most powerful": Peter Drucker, *The Practice of Management* (New York: Harper & Brothers, 2007), 242.

Many leaders and businesspeople behave: B. Garvey, P. Sokes, and D. Megginson, *Coaching and Mentoring: Theory and Practice* (London: Sage Publications, 2008).

how many leaders think and talk about the workplace: P. Shaw, *Changing Conversations in Organizations: Learning and Knowledge Creation* (London: Routledge, 2002).

Instead of an "if this, then that" kind of thinking: Ralph D. Stacey, *Complexity and Organizational Reality: Uncertainty and the Need to Rethink Management after the Collapse of Investment Capitalism* (New York: Routledge, 2010).

an approach of "if this, then maybe": F. Westley, B. Zimmerman, and M. Patton, *Getting to Maybe* (Toronto: Vintage Canada, 2009).

often attributed to Mike Tyson: A simple Google search online will tell you that the Mike Tyson quote is a version of what Helmuth von Moltke the Elder, credited with creating new approaches to directing armies, said in 1872: "No plan of operations extends with certainty beyond the first encounter with the enemy's main strength" (or "no plan survives contact with the enemy").

think of organizations as a conversation: Shaw, *Changing Conversations.*

Chapter 3

distinction between simple, complicated, and complex problems: Westley, Zimmerman, and Patton, *Getting to Maybe*.

In her book, Edmondson tells the story: A. Edmondson, *Teaming: How Organizations Learn, Innovate, and Compete in the Knowledge Economy* (San Francisco: Jossey-Bass, 2012).

they did not enjoy "psychological safety": Psychological safety can be defined as a climate in which people are comfortable expressing and being themselves. When people have psychological safety at work, they feel comfortable sharing concerns and mistakes without fear of embarrassment or retribution. See p. xvi in Amy Edmondson's book, *The Fearless Organization: Creating Psychological Safety in the Workplace for Learning, Innovation, and Growth* (Hoboken, NJ: John Wiley & Sons, 2019).

"helping the grapes realize their destiny": Eric Asimov, "From Ontario, Cool-Climate Wines of Beauty and Vision," *New York Times*, January 16, 2018, nytimes.com/2018/01/16/dining/drinks/wine-ontario-pearl-morissette.html.

should be thought of as a temporary holding position: Garvey, Sokes, and Megginson, *Coaching and Mentoring*.

Chapter 4

understanding where you are most likely to succeed: A.G. Lafley and R. Martin, *Playing to Win: How Strategy Really Works* (Boston: Harvard Business Review Press, 2013).

positions you on a playing field: Roger Martin, "A Plan Is Not a Strategy," posted June 29, 2022, *Harvard Business Review*, YouTube, 9:31, youtu.be/iuYlGRnc7J8.

group of wolves was reintroduced to Yellowstone National Park: "How Wolves Change Rivers," posted February 13, 2014, Sustainable Human, YouTube, 4:33, youtu.be/ysa5OBhXz-Q.

organizations are not machines but conversations: Shaw, *Changing Conversations*.

make a Canadian wine one of the best in the world: Svetlana Atcheva, brand ambassador for Pearl Morissette, pers comm., November 18, 2022.

change the kinds of questions you ask: J. López, *Society and its Metaphors: Language, Social Theory and Social Structure* (London: Continuum, 2003).

Chapter 5

the future drives the present: This concept is something I learned from Norm Trainor. It is a foundational concept we use at The Covenant Group.

anthropologist Mary Douglas called "matter out of place": Mary Douglas, *Purity and Danger: An Analysis of Concepts of Pollution and Taboo* (New York: Routledge, 1966).

Chapter 6

Rihanna grew her brand Fenty Beauty: Madeline Berg, "Fenty's Fortune: Rihanna Is Now Officially a Billionaire," *Forbes*, August 4, 2021, forbes.com/sites/maddieberg/2021/08/04/fentys-fortune-rihanna-is-now-officially-a-billionaire.

success rates for in vitro fertilization (IVF) clinics: In his book, *Breaking Bad Habits: Defy Industry Norms and Reinvigorate Your Business* (Boston: Harvard Business Review Press, 2017), Freek Vermeulen, an associate professor of strategy and entrepreneurship at the London Business School, and his colleague, Mihaela Stan, studied how a government-mandated and publicly accessible initiative that became known as the "League Table" evolved into an interesting case study for thinking about strategy and its implications.

"If everything you do needs to work": The *Wired* article no longer exists online, but you can find the quote in Eric Jackson's "6 Things Jeff Bezos Knew Back in 1997 that Made Amazon a Gorilla," *Forbes*, November 16, 2011, *forbes.com/sites/ericjackson/2011/11/16/6-things-jeff-bezos-knew-back-in-1997-that-made-amazon-a-gorilla.*

Patagonia's mission statement: "Explanation of Patagonia Mission Statement and Vision Statement," Visionary Businessperson, visionarybusinessperson.com/Patagonia; "Earth Is Now Our Only Shareholder," patagonia.com/ownership.

popularized the "what must be true" question: Lafley and Martin, *Playing to Win*; see also Martin's *A New Way to Think*.

Chapter 8

We all have golden apples in our lives: I was reintroduced to this story many years ago when I read the wonderful book *Radical Focus: Achieving Your Most Important Goals with Objectives and Key Results* by Christina R. Wodtke (Palo Alto, CA: Cucina Media, 2021).

He told the WSJ that one of his main guidelines: Bezos's second guideline is that he has three priorities that inform his daily decisions. If you ever learn what those priorities are, let me know. Bezos is known for being secretive, and I have never found a reliable source for this.

Chapter 9

How big do you want to become: David B. Falk, "Lessons From the Man Who Helped Make Michael Jordon," Covenant Group, November 9, 2021, covenantgroup.com/lessons-from-the-man-who-helped-make-michael-jordan.

they often came to appreciate that small can be beautiful: Bo Burlingham, *Small Giants: Companies That Choose to Be Great Instead of Big* (10th ann. ed.) (New York: Portfolio/Penguin, 2016).

Chapter 11

business owners in the Dominican Republic: Alejandro Drexler, Greg Fischer, and Antoinette Schoar, "Keeping It Simple: Financial Literacy and Rules of Thumb," *American Economic Journal: Applied Economics* 6, no. 2 (2014): 1-31.

the case of St. John's Regional Health Center: Sendhil Mullainathan and Eldar Shafir, *Scarcity: Why Having Too Little Means So Much* (New York: Picador, 2013), 183.

SOURCES AND RESOURCES

M Y HOPE is you go out into the world and change the course of rivers. I have created a landing page where you will find downloadable resources and videos to help you navigate the Strategy Quadrant. Additionally, if you wish to join a community of people who are using these tools to transform their lives, you can reach out to us at keitademming.com. Let's all work together to ensure we all know how we are going to bell the cat.

Complexity

Edgeware: Insights from Complexity Science for Health Care Leaders by Brenda Zimmerman, Curt Lindberg, and Paul Plsek
For a primer on complexity thinking, this is one of the best resources that serve as an introduction to complexity thinking.

Rethinking Management: Radical Insights from the Complexity Sciences by Chris Mowles
This is a highly academic book that is more like a textbook. If, however, you are looking for a resource that gets you to rethink your assumptions about business management, this is it.

Complexity and Organizational Reality: Uncertainty and the Need to Rethink Management after the Collapse of Investment Capitalism by Ralph D. Stacey

For a thought-provoking analysis of the inadequacies of traditional approaches to management, this is the book to read. The author emphasizes the deep implications of a world characterized by emergence and uncertainty and suggests more holistic approaches to change that are based on the reality of organizations.

Coaching and Mentoring: Theory and Practice by Robert Garvey, Paul Stokes, and David Megginson

Although this is a book about coaching, these authors situate coaching in the context of complexity. It is the first place I was introduced to the idea that strategy should be viewed as a temporary holding position.

Strategy

A New Way to Think: Your Guide to Superior Management Effectiveness by Roger L. Martin

Roger Martin is such a great thinker, and this book brings together some of the most important ideas around effective management. Although I recommend reading the entire book, if you are pressed for time, you can simply read the chapters that are most relevant to you.

Playing to Win: How Strategy Really Works by A.G. Lafley and Roger L. Martin

The question "Where are you going to play to win?" is now well-used in strategic thinking. This book serves as the foundation for much of that thinking and is well worth the time.

Masters of War: History's Greatest Strategic Thinkers by Andrew R. Wilson and Michael I. Handel
This is a classic book about war strategies that offers a comprehensive and invaluable review of some of the greatest war strategists and theorists. However, it will not give you takeaways you can apply in your business, so read it as background rather than a working manual. I have only ever found it as an audiobook, which includes a downloadable PDF.

Simple Guidelines

Simple Rules: How to Thrive in a Complex World by Donald Sull and Kathleen M. Eisenhardt
Start with this book for an overview of the impact and importance of simple rules and guidelines. The authors do an excellent job of making the content relevant, applicable, and practical to its readers.

Six Simple Rules: How to Manage Complexity without Getting Complicated by Yves Morieux and Peter Tollman
If you are curious about how you might apply complexity in your organization or some of the underlying causes of complexity, then this is the book to read. The authors make a compelling case for how we often create more complexity in our traditional approaches to management, and offer six rules for taming complexity in your organization.

Risk Savvy: How to Make Good Decisions by Gerd Gigerenzer
Although this book is primarily about risk, the author does a great job of demonstrating how rules of thumb and simple guidelines can be more effective than complex approaches. Ultimately, this book is about helping you make better decisions

and argues that simple guidelines are one of our best tools for improving decision making.

Organizations as Conversations

Changing Conversations in Organizations: A Complexity Approach to Change by Patricia Shaw
This book argues for a holistic approach to organizational change. The author argues that lasting change requires respecting more emergent approaches. This is the book that prompted me to view organizations as conversations and not machines. It is a compelling read and provides a mix of tools and approaches to changing conversations in organizations.

Conversations for Action and Collected Essays: Instilling a Culture of Commitment in Working Relationships by Fernando Flores and Maria Flores Letelier (Editor)
This book argues that we build the future through conversations. If you are looking for a framework that will help you conduct conversation that leads to action, then this is a great place to start. Though it's not an easy read, its content is incredibly valuable.

Decisive: How to Make Better Choices in Life and Work by Chip Heath and Dan Heath
Strategy and conversations are ultimately about decision making. This book provides you with a simple framework to help you make better choices in life and in business. For a practical approach to decision making, this book would be helpful.

Creating Better Organizations

The Decision Book: Fifty Models for Strategic Thinking by Mikael Krogerus and Roman Tschappeler
I often use this quick read as a reference point when developing my own frameworks and models.

BE 2.0 *(Beyond Entrepreneurship 2.0): Turning Your Business into an Enduring Great Company* by Jim Collins and William Lazier
I love the idea of building great companies, and for me this book offers some of the best thinking around how to build successful organizations. The case studies and examples offer actionable insights for entrepreneurs and leaders.

Sensemaking: The Power of the Humanities in the Age of the Algorithm by Christian Madsbjerg
In our rapidly changing world, the study of humanities is becoming more important. The author does an excellent job of making the case for humanities in the world of business. In a world so focused on big data and abstraction, we could all benefit from Christian Madsbjerg's reminder to focus on human interactions as a way to spur innovation and strategy.

The Fearless Organization: Creating Psychological Safety in the Workplace for Learning, Innovation, and Growth by Amy C. Edmondson
Ever since Google published their study that found that psychological safety is the largest contributing factor to high-performing teams, Amy Edmondson's work has grown in popularity. Creating psychological safety is perhaps one of the most important skills leaders and entrepreneurs can learn to foster. Although I recommend all of Edmondson's books, this one does an excellent job of bringing all her previous work into one great resource.

The 360° Corporation: From Stakeholder Trade-offs to Transformation by Sarah Kaplan

I long for a world where all organizations contribute to a thriving society. This book offers one of the most compelling arguments and guides for how companies can change their business model to meet the needs and perspectives of all their stakeholders. We must move beyond minimizing harm and maximizing shareholder returns. This is perhaps one of the most practical books in that space.

ABOUT
THE AUTHOR

WHEN I was sixteen, my mother and I took a trip to New York City. She says that as I walked the streets of Manhattan, tugging on her coat, I looked her in the eye and said, "One day I will be teaching people leadership and change in a city like this." For a teenager who grew up on the islands of Trinidad and Tobago, the lights and buildings of New York were nothing but inspiring. The trouble was that I was a high school dropout who was written off by his teachers as an athlete with little to no academic potential.

Today, I have a PhD in Adult Education and Workplace Learning. Companies connect with me to help them accelerate learning, leadership, and strategic direction, and to design customized workshops or programs for strategic business units. Who would have imagined that this kid from the Caribbean could become a sought-after educator and coach?

Now, as an award-winning educator and coach, I work to transform companies into places and spaces that are idea-driven and people-centred. The more we learn from others, the more likely we are to find our own journey a little bit easier. This is what drives my passion for the work I do at The Covenant Group, where I design training programs and coach clients to meet their strategic goals and build their businesses.

I like to think of myself as someone who helps people become better businesspeople and better people in business. This role is truly meaningful because I help people enjoy their work and thrive so that they aren't just more productive, they're happier.

One of my proudest achievements outside of my work is fostering community. I co-built and developed TEDxPortof-Spain, a local version of the popular TED ideas festival. It was one of the most successful TEDx events in the world, and I am proud that everyone involved knew they had a say in the vision. Lasting success comes from leading with people, not simply managing them.

T HE COVENANT GROUP has coached tens of thousands of leaders, entrepreneurs, and organizations in how to develop new lines of business or overcome complex problems that stand in the way of success.

Building any new training or workshop starts with people first. This is what I love about what I do—drawing on my academic research on innovation and organizational change and translating it into tools, coaching, and consulting to help clients take immediate action and generate results. I also leverage technology and user experience design to help our clients move the needle by:

- developing programs and products to add value to high-performing organizations

- delivering proven products and coaching clients through effective learning experiences

- adapting internal processes that ensure our teams and clients excel

Programs

The Covenant Group offers high-performing business coaching programs designed to enhance your value proposition by addressing the issues you and your team experience in building your business. We build on what you already know and do to redefine your level of performance, helping you maximize strengths and resources. The focus is on implementation. You gain membership into a diverse network of capabilities that will enrich your business.

Business Builder Playbook

When you join this program, you get access to a peer-to-peer business and leadership coaching program that gives you a roadmap to grow your business and achieve and sustain optimal performance. Get the guidance you need at every step of your journey.

The Elite Entrepreneur

This is an exclusive peer-to-peer business coaching program designed for highly successful entrepreneurs and business leaders. If you think you qualify for this program, reach out and we can have a conversation. For many executives and entrepreneurs, executing their business plan is a serious challenge. This program helps you develop a sound business strategy and effectively put it into action. The program helps move you from knowing to doing, and we will work with you to solve the specific and unique challenges to realizing your desired future.

Executive Coaching

Our one-on-one coaching follows a simple process flow as outlined below.

1 Initial Interview

We believe very strongly in an initial interview between the coaching candidate and the coach. Ideal candidates express a desire to learn new ways of doing things and want to be exposed to new approaches to achieving their desired future.

In addition, wanting to learn something new is not the same as wanting to embrace change; one expresses intellectual curiosity, the other self-analysis and self-efficacy. Ideal candidates for Executive Coaching are looking to address the challenges they face in their business and willing to question their methods. They want to implement change in how they do business to achieve and sustain peak performance.

2   Coaching

The purpose is to address the issues and challenges in your business and help keep you accountable to ensure implementation. Coaching is designed to support and challenge you as you work to realize your desired future. While many of our clients have been engaged with our programs for a number of years, we ask that you commit to twelve months of coaching initially.

3   Forward Planning

At each six-month interval, we summarize our progress to date and create a forward-looking plan to keep you on track.

Strategy Lab

This is a facilitated experience of the Strategy Quadrant. We meet with you to determine the scope, objectives, and timelines. Then we design a learning journey for your team. Next, we develop a plan and work with you to execute your strategy. We act as lab facilitators and implementation coaches as you learn how to play and win.

Connect with Me

We would love to hear how the ideas presented in this book help you in the real world. To share your Strategy Quadrant stories, please connect with me at keitademming.com. You can also find me on Twitter or Instagram using the handle @kdemming and the hashtag #StrategytoAction. I am also available on LinkedIn.

Printed in the USA
CPSIA information can be obtained
at www.ICGtesting.com
JSHW020444100923
48057JS00004B/155